RAILWAYS
of the
YORKSHIRE DALES

Compiled by
MICHAEL BLAKEMORE

In the same series:
RAILWAYS OF THE NORTH YORK MOORS

Atlantic Publishers
Trevithick House, West End, Penryn, Cornwall TR10 8HE

ISBN: 1 902827 02 3

Design and layout: BARNABUS DESIGN & REPRO, TRURO

Printed by THE AMADEUS PRESS LTD., BRADFORD

British Cataloguing in Publication Data
A catalogue for this book is available from the British Library

CONTENTS

The 'Cream Special' at Northallerton on 26th April 1927. Dairymen propel the four-wheel trolley carrying milk churns and cream cans from the Wensleydale Pure Milk Society bottling plant for return to the Dales stations. A red flag on a pole denotes its presence instead of the more usual front and tail lamps! (NRM/Household collection 327)

INTRODUCTION

Mention 'Yorkshire' and the word 'Dales' often springs immediately to mind to accompany it – the two seem to go together. Yet it would be wrong to think of the Yorkshire Dales as a single entity; they are more a family of constituent members, some large, some small and little-known, each with its own identity and geographical character. The Dales embrace a wide area lying between the Pennines and the Vale of York; on the eastern slopes of the Pennines rise the rivers which form the dales as they make their way, joining others, ultimately to the sea. To the south west Wharfedale stretches away from the industrial towns and cities of the West Riding and is in considerable contrast to the more northerly and easterly dales of the Wensley and the Swale where the scenery is less rugged, more agricultural.

Whilst large parts of the smaller dales have been undisturbed by the coming of railways, most of the larger dales were opened up to rail travel either by terminating branch lines or by cross-country routes connected to other lines at either end. Not all the Dales railways were meandering byways, for on both the western and eastern fringes of the area important main lines forged routes to the north and south. On the west that most renowned of main lines, the Midland Railway's Settle—Carlisle route, was built in the boldest of gestures to form an integral part of its line from London to Carlisle. Over to the east the Leeds Northern line from Leeds to Northallerton, via Harrogate and Ripon, carried a Pullman service to Scotland and the important expresses between Liverpool and Newcastle.

One of the longest Dales branches connected them at Northallerton and Hawes Junction, though serving no large population centres along the way. Others served towns of some size and importance such as Richmond and Ilkley or market towns like Pateley Bridge and Masham. Local people were taken to work, to market, to fairs and holidays, to war, while increasingly in later years visitors were brought into the Dales to explore what HRH The Prince of Wales has described as "one of the most treasured landscapes in Britain".

As with so many secondary railways, those of the Yorkshire Dales have not fared too well with the passing of time. The Grassington branch passenger service ceased in 1930, the Wensleydale and Pateley Bridge branches followed during the 1950s and the sweeping cuts of the 1960s further took their toll, including the main line through Ripon.

But all is not gloom, by any means. The Settle–Carlisle line, for so much of the 1980s neglected and threatened with closure, was reprieved and is now enjoying a revival in fortunes, with recent refurbishment of track having been undertaken; its cheery stations and increased traffic are the positive indications of how a railway can be turned round. Another encouraging development during the 1990s was the electrification of the routes from Leeds and Bradford to Skipton and Ilkley; new trains are being introduced and the frequent services appear to be well patronised. And there may be more to come; across in Wensleydale campaigners are endeavouring to restore train services on a line which survived to carry freight for another 40 years after its closure to passengers.

The full story of the Yorkshire Dales railways has been told expertly and in detail elsewhere. This book seeks only to provide a pictorial survey of the railway scene in this favourite part of the White Rose county – past and recent. My thanks are particularly due to David Beeken, John Edgington and Gavin Morrison for their help with photographs and to all those others – sometimes unknown – whose cameras recorded the views we now offer.

MICHAEL BLAKEMORE
January 2001

WHARFEDALE

Wharfedale takes Yorkshire from the urban and industrial areas of Leeds and Bradford to the moors above Ilkley, Otley and Skipton. Heading north through either extemity of Wharfedale were two main lines — the Midland Railway's line from Leeds to Skipton and the Leeds & Thirsk (later the Leeds Northern then the North Eastern) route through Harrogate. Proposals for a line to connect them were put forward during the 'Railway Mania', the most notable being the Lancashire & Yorkshire North Eastern Railway which saw itself running from Skipton to Wetherby and York. Nothing of substance arose from this, even after the section east of a junction with the Leeds & Thirsk at Arthington had been abandoned by agreement with the latter. Subsequently the Leeds Northern arranged with private operators to provide 'omnibus' connections from Ilkley and Otley to Arthington.

The lack of mineral resources in Wharfedale had not inspired transport developments in the area and since nothing had come of various other abortive schemes, in 1859 local parties made approaches to both the Midland and the North Eastern which had hitherto been hostile to independent companies penetrating their territories. The result was that they agreed for once to work together to build a line through Wharfedale. The NER would build a line from Arthington to Otley, from there to Ilkley would be a joint undertaking, then the MR would provide a link from its route at Apperley to a double-ended junction at Burley. The Otley—Arthington section was opened on 1st February 1865, the rest of the route following on 1st August.

The railway was soon stimulating a population growth in places such as Ilkley and Otley; it even spurred the development of Ilkey as a health resort after the water had been found to contain sulphur efficacious in the treating of certain skin diseases.

Further additions to the Wharfedale railway network were inevitable. Firstly, in 1876 the MR opened a link from Shipley to Esholt Junction, south of Guiseley, which gave a direct route for trains from Bradford to Otley and Ilkley and on through to Harrogate. Given the growing popularity of the area of Wharfedale around Bolton Abbey, an extension of the railway from Ilkley to Skipton was a further logical move and this was achieved by the Midland on 1st October 1888. Bolton Abbey soon became a popular destination for excursions, while a range of through trains travelled via the Otley route, notably an inter-war service between Bradford and Newcastle.

The cuts of the 'Beeching Axe' did not miss Wharfedale and the Arthington—Ilkley—Skipton route was closed on 22nd March 1965. Ilkley, however, remained rail-served by the line from Apperley Junction and the Shipley—Guiseley branch, moreover, they survived to see electrification in the 1990s! The Aire Valley electrification scheme was completed in 1995 and took in the Leeds—Skipton route together with the branches to Bradford Forster Square and Ilkley. A frequent service of electric trains now plies between these places and it is encouraging to see them well patronised.

A belated railway arrival in Wharfedale was the Grassington branch. Its origins, though, lay in grandiose schemes in the 1840s to create a new through route between Lancashire and the North East. The Liverpool, Manchester & Newcastle upon Tyne Railway of 1846 got nowhere, nor did othe[r] propsals in the 1860s and 1880s, then in 1895 the Yorkshire Dale[s] Railway proposed a line from Embsay and Hellifield through upper Wharfedale and Coverdale to Darlington. This was far too ambitious a scheme for such a late date, so the company settled for an initial branch from Embsay to Grassington whilst doubtles[s] harbouring thoughts of future extension.

The branch was opened on 29th July 1902 and was worked from the outset by the Midland, though the Yorkshire Dale[s] Railway retained its nominal independence until the Grouping. Grassington remained the terminus; it was, in fact, named Grassington & Threshfield since it was situated mid-wa[y] between the two. Such an inconvenient location no doub[t] contributed to a lack of patronage and the branch passenge[r] service fell by the wayside as early as 22nd September 1930. Grassington nevertheless remained a favourite destination fo[r] excursions, particularly for ramblers, and a goods servic[e] continued until 11th August 1969. That, however, was still no[t] the end of the Grassington branch as a large limestone works [at] Swinden continues to generate traffic to this day.

Finally, mention must be made of the fact that the name Yorkshire Dales Railway lives on in the form of a preservation society based at Embsay which in 1979 re-opened a short stretch of the Skipton–Ilkley line. Although not the biggest or most famous of preserved railways, it extended its track to give a round steam-hauled trip of three miles and in 1998 opened a further extension to Bolton Abbey where it built a splendid re-creation of the Midland Railway station.

A busy moment at Otley's sizeable station in Edwardian days. A North Eastern Railway Harrogate train is on the left, while the rear of a Midland train can be glimpsed on the right.

An LNER train on the Midland route from Apperley Junction — D20 4-4-0 No.2393 heads a Leeds—Ilkley express through Menston on 11th June 1947. (H.C. Casserley)

The ubiquitous North Eastern Railway G5 0-4-4Ts could be seen on the Leeds—Ilkley via Arthington trains. An unidentified specimen is pictured in the woods near Ben Rhydding c1950. (G.T.G. Findley)

The terminal platforms at Ilkley during the 1930s — Midland 2P 4-4-0 No.562 awaits departure running tender-first probably to Bradford.

The Aire Valley electrification in 1995 was a bold step forward but no new rolling stock was provided to herald the new age. Instead Class 308 electric multiple units, built in 1961 for the London, Tilbury & Southend lines but made redundant there, were transferred north for a further lease of life. Here is a pair of three-car sets at Ilkley on 31st August 1995. Note the Midland Railway quarter-mile post on the station wall, denoting 211¼ miles from St. Pancras.
(T.J. Edgington)

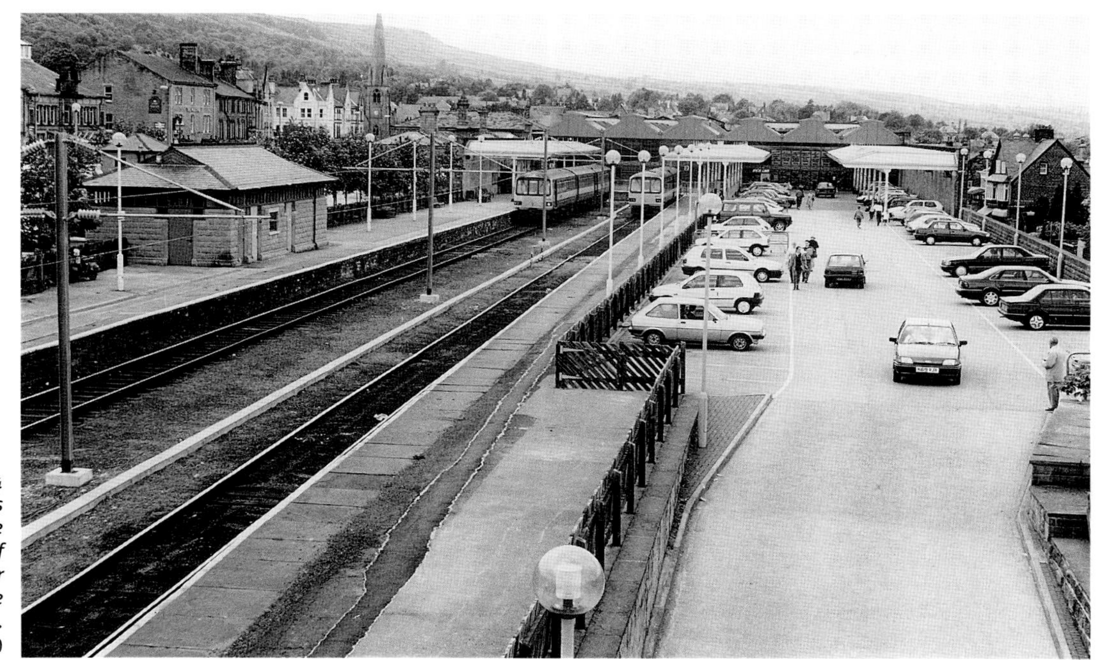

Ilkley station on 28th May 1994 with 'Pacer' diesel units for Leeds (left) and Bradford Forster Square (right). Occupying the trackbed of the former through lines is a car park but a pleasing touch is the retention of the platform canopies.
(T.J. Edgington)

Ilkley station consisted of two terminal platforms (the original Otley & Ilkley Joint Line terminus) and two through platforms for trains on the Midland route to Skipton. LMS 'Patriot' 4-6-0 No.45505 The Royal Army Ordnance Corps *heads out of Ilkley towards Skipton with a return excursion to Whaley Bridge on 15th May 1955. Following closure of the Skipton route the bridge over the road has been removed.*

A joint MR/NER engine shed was provided at Ilkley in 1866, originally close to the station where it was subject to complaints about smoke nuisance. With the opening of the Skipton line, the opportunity was taken to move the depot to a new site north of the station in 1892. Engines were outstationed from Leeds (Neville Hill) and Bradford (Manningham). As a sub-shed of Manningham, Ilkley depot closed on 5th January 1959 when diesel units took over local services. Resident on 22nd April 1956 were two Stanier LMS 2-6-2Ts Nos.40147 and 40114 and an ex-LYR 2-4-2T No.50636. (F.W. Smith)

In LMS days Lancashire & Yorkshire Railway 2-4-2 radial tanks infiltrated Wharfedale and examples could be found shedded at Manningham and Ilkley into BR days. Here is No.10880 on a local at Bolton Abbey.

Embsay Junction, with the Midland Railway signal box positioned between the Grassington branch diverging to the left and the main line to Bolton Abbey and Ilkley.

Limestone has been despatched from Swinden Quarry, near Rylstone, since the opening of the Grassington branch. Latterly, steam motive power was provided by BR Class 4 4-6-0s from Skipton and then Carnforth depots. In a bare landscape awaiting the coming of spring, No.75026 makes its way towards Grassington with a freight, including coal hoppers, on 17th March 1967. (Gavin Morrison)

Ilkley station on 30th July 1966 and a Leeds train waits at Platform 3, one of the now abandoned through platforms. Note the portable steps to compensate for the low platform. (Colour-Rail)

A Skipton—Ilkley DMU (with the early yellow 'whiskers' which pre-dated yellow visibility panels) approaches Bolton Abbey station in August 1964. (Colour-Rail)

Grassington c1905, immaculate and still new-looking after its opening only three years earlier. The station seats have the full name 'Grassington and Threshfield' taking up their entire length!

A poignant photograph at Grassington station on 21st September 1914. Only six weeks into what was to be known as the 'Great War' and these young recruits, full of patriotism and optimism, have answered the call to arms and are off to join the colours. One wonders how many would return.....

Although the Grassington branch lost its passenger services in 1930, excursions — particularly ramblers' specials — continued to make occasional visits. LMS 4F 0-6-0 No.44041 prepares to leave with the empty stock of a ramblers' excursion from Bradford in April 1950. (David Joy collection)

Goods traffic to Grassington continued until 1969. Here is a 4F 0-6-0 shunting on a damp Dales day amid some fine signals; there are two Midland lower quadrants and a bracket in the distance, while an LMS or BR upper quadrant shunting arm has been installed on a MR yard signal post. (David Joy collection)

ABOVE: *An established feature of the preserved Yorkshire Dales Railway's motive power policy has been the use of industrial locomotives. Here at Embsay station in 1986 is a train double-headed by a pair of 0-6-0STs* Slough Estates No.3 *(built by Hudswell, Clarke & Co. in 1939) and NCB No.S134* Wheldale *(built by the Hunslet Engine Co. in 1944 for the War Department and later used at Primrose Hill Colliery, Swillington, and Wheldale Colliery, near Castleford).* (T.J. Edgington)

RIGHT: *The restored LNER K4 2-6-0 No.3442* The Great Marquess *hea*
'The Dalesman' railtour between Otley and Burley-in-Wharfedale
4th May 1963. On the right can be seen the Midland route via Menst
and Guiseley to the Aire Valley main line. (Derek Penn

RCTS
3442
L N E R

Since 1969 the limestone aggregates traffic has kept the remaining stretch of the Grassington branch open between Skipton and Rylstone. Between 1970 and 1973 Swinden Quarry (by then owned by Tilcon-Tilling Construction Services Ltd.) was modernised and expanded to double its output, with new hopper wagons constructed. On 30th July 1992 BR Class 60 No.60 095 Crib Goch *rounds the curve to the site of the former Embsay Junction with the 10.16 Swinden—Hull train.* (Gavin Morrison)

NIDDERDALE

To the east of Nidderdale passed a now-vanished main line — the Leeds Northern route from Harrogate through Ripon to Northallerton — along which expresses such as those running cross-country from Liverpool to Newcastle used to thunder. This originated as the Leeds & Thirsk Railway, authorised in 1845, and soon after construction started it had its eyes on extensions to the north via Northallerton and Yarm to join the Stockton & Hartlepool Railway. Parliamentary powers were sought but George Hudson exerted pressure to have the stretch between Melmerby and Northallerton dropped from the scheme so that trains would use his Great North of England Railway between Thirsk and Northallerton.

The railway was opened between Ripon and Thirsk on 31st May 1848; Weeton to Wormald Green was ready for opening on 1st September 1848, followed by the intermediate link from Wormald Green to Ripon on 13th September. Opening of the route down to Leeds awaited the completion of the 3,791yds-long Bramhope Tunnel and the entire line was not open throughout until 9th July 1849.

The Leeds & Thirsk had very soon looked again at extending north from Melmerby to Northallerton and obtained powers to do so in 1848. In 1851 the company changed its name to the Leeds Northern Railway and its main line became an important through route. However, by the 1960s British Railways was no longer regarding it as essential and services north of Harrogate were withdrawn on 6th March 1967.

Leading off the Leeds Northern a delightful branch line penetrated into Nidderdale itself. The possibility of a branch to Pateley Bridge had been raised by the Leeds & Thirsk but after obtaining Parliamentary authority it allowed the powers to lapse. It was left to the North Eastern Railway to revive the proposal and the branch from a junction at Nidd, just north of Harrogate, was opened on 1st May 1862.

The Pateley Bridge branch (14½ miles from Harrogate) made its contribution to life in the dale until competition from motor buses proved too great and it became an early British Railways closure victim. Passenger services were withdrawn on 2nd April 1951, though goods traffic continued until 31st October 1964.

Pateley Bridge was, however, by no means the end of railway penetration into Nidderdale; further up the dale was a source of perhaps even greater railway interest. To provide further reliable water supplies for its growing city, Bradford Corporation at the end of the nineteenth century was planning to construct reservoirs in Nidderdale; the first, the Gouthwaite Compensation Reservoir, was completed in 1901. In that year a Light Railway Order had been granted for a 2ft 6in gauge line from Pateley Bridge to Lofthouse to open up the northern extremity of Nidderdale. When by 1904 nothing had been done about it, Bradford Corporation decided to take over powers for the line to use in connection with its next programme of reservoir building. Construction of the Nidd Valley Light Railway began in July 1904 when a civic party from Bradford travelled on the 3ft works railway already existing between Lofthouse and Angram. This was extended to Pateley Bridge that year but in May the Board of Trade had agreed to its conversion to standard gauge. This was undertaken in 1906/7 which then enabled wagonloads of construction material to be worked through from the NER.

Bradford Corporation had also acquired an obligation to provide a passenger service between Pateley Bridge and Lofthouse, a distance of 6¼ miles, and this was formally inaugurated on 11th September 1907. The line beyond Lofthouse was used only to convey men and materials for the construction of the reservoirs. After eleven years the Angram reservoir was finished but it was another five years before work started on the next, Scar House.

The NVLR's passenger service did not last long — just over 22 years. It was discontinued from 1st January 1930, though goods traffic continued to the Scar House reservoir site. Soon after the reservoir had been completed in 1936, the railway was closed and dismantled.

On 30th May 1967 LMS 'Jubilee' 4-6-0 No.45562 Alberta *was unexpectedly used to head a Royal Train, conveying the Duke of Edinburgh, from York to Nidd Bridge. After the Duke had alighted, No.45562 took the train forward to Ripon in order to run round and is seen at Wormald Green, three months after the line had closed to passengers. This was the last steam-hauled Royal Train.* (Gavin Morrison)

Pullman days on the Leeds Northern — BR 'Deltic' No.D9006 (later named The Fife and Forfar Yeomanry) *crosses the Ure at Ripon with the down 'Queen of Scots' c1962.* (Colour-Rail DE447)

LEFT: *Another view of the surprise 'Jubilee'-hauled Royal Train working on 30th May 1967. No.45562* Alberta *has run round the stock at Ripon before returning to York.* (Gavin Morrison)

BELOW: *The photographer has recorded a rather special 'cop' at Ripon in May 1935 in the distinctive shape of the unique Class W1 ' Hush-Hush' 4-6-4 No.10000, fitted with water tube boiler, on the 4.17pm Newcastle—Liverpool. This experimental locomotive had just returned to service after modifications at Darlington Works to fit a Kylchap exhaust and was working from Leeds Neville Hill shed on expresses to Newcastle.* (J.W. Hague/D.V. Beeken collection)

Another reminder of when main line expresses between Leeds and the North East used the Leeds Northern line through Ripon. A4 Pacific No.4494 Osprey *is seen heading north, wearing the standard apple green livery it carried from new in August 1937 to October 1938 when it was repainted garter blue. A further change in 1942 saw it renamed* Andrew K. McCosh. (J.W. Hague/D.V. Beeken collection)

Nidderdale Agricultural Show

Mon 22nd Sept

Cheap Day Tickets

will be issued to Pateley Bridge at ordinary single fare for the return journey from all stations within a radius of 60 miles

Available any train

FOR CONDITIONS OF ISSUE SEE OTHER SIDE.

Tickets, bills and all particulars can be obtained at the Stations, also at the usual Town Offices. For further information apply to the District Passenger Managers at Leeds (Tel. No. 20615) and York (Tel. No. 2264).

TICKETS CAN BE OBTAINED IN ADVANCE

London & North Eastern Railway

LEEDS Sept 1930 — 1712—Petty & Sons (Leeds) Ltd—7,000

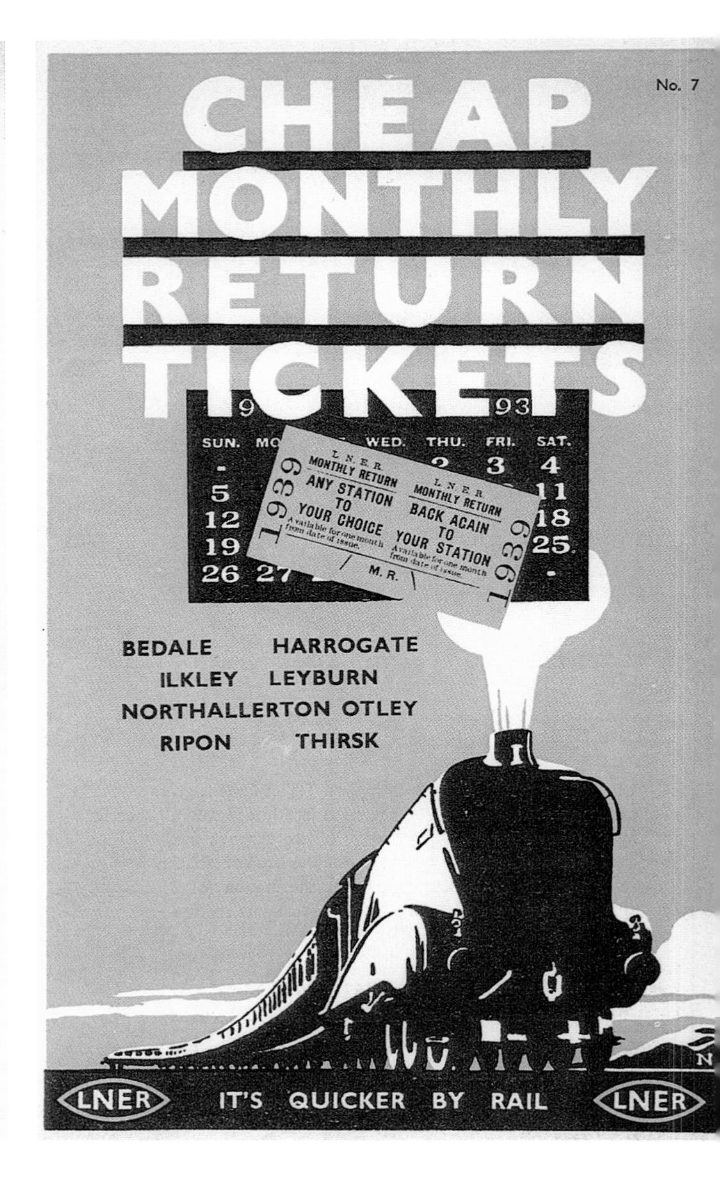

A 1930 handbill for cheap travel on the Pateley Bridge branch.

The LNER had a flair for publicity and made good use of stylistic representations of its A4 streamliners and the 1937 'Coronation' streamlined train. Passengers beginning their journeys at some of these Dales stations would not, however, find anything quite so exotic awaiting them! (D. V. Beeken collection)

The NER's Class Z Atlantics were fine-looking machines and as LNER Class C7 here is No.710 leaving Ripon with a down pre-war express.
(J.W. Hague/D.V. Beeken collection)

A North Eastern Railway Class R 4-4-0 — LNER Class D20 — No.2384 calls at Ripon with an up local service cNovember 1948. (J.W. Hague/D.V. Beeken collection)

A3 No.60086 Gainsborough *races south through Melmerby in the early 1950s. On the left the Masham branch curves away, the platform fenced off following its closure to passengers some twenty years previously.*
(J.W. Hague/D.V. Beeken collection)

The 'Queen of Scots' Pullman (King's Cross—Leeds—Edinburgh—Glasgow) was the prestige train on the Leeds Northern route. On 12th July 1950 A3 No.60084 Trigo *was in charge of the up train passing Middleton Lane, Melmerby.*
(J.W. Hague/D.V. Beeken collection)

Hurrying through the hayfields at Monkton Moor, A3 No.60081 Shotover *has the assistance of D20 4-4-0 No.62378 (which has sustained a scorched smokebox door) on a Newcastle to Liverpool express during the early 1950s.*
(J.W. Hague/D.V. Beeken collection)

Pateley Bridge station on 8th April 1950 finds G5 0-4-4T No.67284 just arrived on the 1.35pm from Harrogate. The glazed conservatory-type structure was an unusual feature of this branch terminus. (T.J. Edgington)

No.67284 again on the same train as in the previous picture, this time blowing off steam at Dacre as it waits for passengers to unload themselves and their belongings. This was the busiest intermediate station on the branch, handling timber, agricultural produce and high-grade sand.

Seen at Lofthouse on the Nidd Valley Light Railway is the Kerr, Stuart steam railmotor built for the Great Western Railway in 1905 and bought by Bradford Corporation in 1921. It was named Hill *in honour of Sir James Hill, a long-serving member of the waterworks committee and Lord Mayor of Bradford in 1908/9.*

4-4-0T Holdsworth *was acquired for use on the NVLR in 1906. Built by Beyer, Peacock & Co. in 1866, it was previously Metropolitan Railway No.20. It is seen outside the NER roundhouse at York, as repainted by the Metropolitan at Neasen, on its way to its new home. The engine is named after Alderman W. Holdsworth, chairman of the waterworks committee.*

0-6-0T Milner *was built new for the Nidd Valley by Hudswell, Clarke & Co. in 1909 and was used on the passenger service until replaced by the railmotor in 1921. It then moved to Scar Village for passenger and goods work and was sold in 1934. It took the name of an earlier* Milner, *the other of the pair of Metropolitan 4-4-0Ts which was sold in 1914.*

Blythe *(an Avonside Engine Co. 0-6-0ST built in 1922) and the railmotor are seen outside the two-road shed at Pateley Bridge. The water tank is a delightful Heath Robinson affair, seeming to consist of every bit of construction material around!* (Photomatic)

Lofthouse station en fête *on 11th September 1907 for the opening of the Nidd Valley Light Railway by the Lord Mayor of Bradford. Pateley Bridge is away in the right-hand direction.*

Pictured in 1928, 0-4-0ST Craven, *supplied to Bradford Corporation by Hudswell, Clarke in 1920, amid some of the huge stone blocks hewn from the surrounding hillside for the construction of the Scar House dam.* (Photomatic)

The Scar House reservoir construction site. The stone was mostly quarried locally and the railway brought in huge quantities of cement. Construction began on 5th October 1921; the cost of the project was £2.5 million and the reservoir — 1,054ft above sea level and covering 172 acres — has a capacity of 2,200 million gallons. Overlooking the site is Scar Village containing residential hostels, school, shops, mission church, concert hall, dining rooms and bathrooms. (Photomatic)

A freight for the Scar construction site in 1928 climbs the bank above Lofthouse with Milner *in the lead double-heading with* Blythe*; another pair of locomotives is banking at the rear.* (Photomatic)

The Masham Branch

An Act of Parliament was obtained in 1871 by the North Eastern Railway for a branch just over seven miles long from Melmerby, north of Ripon on the former Leeds Northern main line, to Masham, a small market town on the River Ure. The actual terminus was in Burton-upon-Ure, about ½-mile outside the town and on the opposite bank of the river. Construction of the branch began in 1873 and it opened for traffic on 9th June 1875.

Reservoir construction also played a part in the history of the Masham branch. In 1901 Harrogate Corporation gained authority to build Roundhill Reservoir, some five miles south west of Masham. A construction depot was established at Leighton to which materials were carried by road from Masham station, but damage was soon being caused to the roads. A railway had been established from the Leighton depot to the site of the dam and in 1904 Harrogate Corporation was empowered to extend its line into Masham where the NER provided a transhipment siding from its goods yard.

Once the Roundhill reservoir had been completed in 1910, the works railway was taken over by Leeds Corporation which was building the adjacent Leighton reservoir. The outbreak of war in 1914 put that project into abeyance and the site huts were taken over firstly for military accommodation and then to hold German prisoners-of-war. The Leighton Reservoir was eventually completed in the 1920s, following which the line was abandoned.

As for the Masham branch itself, it became an early victim of a lack of passenger traffic when trains were withdrawn from 1st January 1931. Goods traffic continued to run and there was a considerable upturn in traffic during World War II when the area around Tanfield was chosen as a storage point for ammunition. The volume of munitions grew throughout the war until 76,000 tons were handled, while in the six weeks leading up to D-Day 42 ammunition trains were run.

The local pick-up goods struggled on until 1963 but it seems that by then trade was rather thin. In November 1962 the MP for Darlington complained in the House of Commons that the branch was being kept open just to supply fresh water to the crossing gatehouses and to deliver coal to Masham and Tanfield for sale by the Masham station master (this was a concession with the job going back to NER days). Whatever, time finally ran out for the Masham branch when the goods service was withdrawn on 11th November 1963.

LNER J39 0-6-0 No.64855 is caught in a rural setting overlooked by the village church at Tanfield as it crosses the Ripon to Masham road with a solitary mineral wagon for Masham on 4th March 1953. With such light traffic, it is perhaps surprising that the branch goods continued for another ten years. (J.W. Hague/D.V. Beeken collection)

NER A6 4-6-2T No.9791 trots away from Melmerby with two empty wagons on the Ripon—Masham goods on 4th May 1949. The main line towards Northallerton is in the background.
(J.W. Hague/D.V. Beeken collection)

The following day the same locomotive had a rather better load as it ran back down the branch towards the junction at Melmerby.
(J.W. Hague/D.V. Beeken collection)

An early photograph of Masham station in the 1880s with NER 2-4-0ST No.84 heading the branch train. Station and train do not seem to be short of staff! (NRM 6/01)

0-6-2T Leeds No.1 *was built by the Hunslet Engine Co. and supplied to Leeds Corporation in 1905 for the construction of the Leighton reservoir.*

RIBBLESDALE, DENTDALE AND GARSDALE

No book on the railways of the Yorkshire Dales would be complete without inclusion of the Settle to Carlisle line. It may not entirely fit in with the "Byways" concept of this series, yet for much of its life it has undoubtedly been a secondary route.

This spectacular railway over the Pennines has had a chequered career. Conceived in the late 1860s by the Midland Railway, desperate to have its own access to Scotland, it was almost killed at birth. Apprehensive of the costs of building a trunk route through such inhospitable country, the company patched up an agreement to gain access to Carlisle over the tracks of its old enemy the London & North Western Railway. But a Government fearful of monopolies threw out the abandonment Bill and the Midland was forced to proceed. It says much for the company – and the high ideals of the Victorian age – that it did not indulge in cheese-paring tactics. Instead it built the most magnificent of railways.

The Midland had good reason to be apprehensive. Constructing the line over rain-sodden uplands, once succinctly dismissed by a Dales farmer as "nowt but scenery", proved to be a heroic undertaking. Enormous shanty towns sprang up to house the navvies who for seven long years laboured with pick, shovel, wheelbarrow and precious little else. Construction costs were woefully underestimated and Midland shareholders grew anxious. There was no mood for elaborate ceremony when the line finally opened to passengers on 1st May 1876.

Once the Midland became part of the LMS in 1923, the glory days of the Settle to Carlisle were over. It was now a secondary route, useful for slow-moving freight traffic and the odd express on its way from St Pancras to Glasgow or Edinburgh. Years of decline appeared to be coming to an inevitable conclusion in 1983 when British Rail officially announced its intention to withdraw services.

The upshot was the most bitterly fought closure campaign in railway history. Objections were lodged by no fewer than 22,265 people – and one dog! Matters became highly political and dragged on for years, the line becoming such a focus of attention that passenger numbers increased from 93,000 in 1983 to almost half a million five years later. Finally, in 1989 the Minister of Transport announced a reprieve.

For the second time in Settle-Carlisle history, a railway company was now compelled to spend reluctant millions. Long neglect has been put right, viaducts repaired, stations improved, track renewed and signalling modernised. Heavy freight traffic has returned and the line now carries a more intensive local passenger service than at any time in its history.

The journey is memorable. From Settle the climb up Ribblesdale is on a ruling gradient of 1 in 100 – known to generations of perspiring firemen as the "Long Drag". This is the heart of Three Peaks country, with splendid views of Penyghent, Ingleborough and Whernside. The 1,000ft contour is crossed just before Ribblehead with its famous viaduct – 24 arches soaring over 100 feet above the surrounding moorland and yet utterly dwarfed by the nearby mountains.

The line curves gradually northwards to reach Blea Moor and what is arguably the most remote signal box in Britain. The black hole of 1 mile 869yd Blea Moor tunnel takes the traveller through to a very different landscape: a shelf high above the green floor of Dentdale. Dent station, highest on the line, is four miles distant from the village it purports to serve.

Another tunnel – 1,213yd Rise Hill – leads through to Garsdale, where were situated the highest water troughs in the world. Garsdale station, junction for the Hawes branch (see Wensleydale chapter), once boasted a small engine shed and a unique turntable stockaded as protection against the wind. Passengers becalmed by late-running trains could use a library in the waiting room, while railway staff had a social centre – complete with piano, stage and upholstered seats – beneath the huge water tank.

Garsdale is close to one of the great watersheds of northern England, where the rivers Ure and Eden rise within yards of one another. Here too is the line's 1,169ft summit, beyond which it leaves the rugged Yorkshire Dales and descends into the softer surroundings of the Eden Valley.

A photograph that bears all the hallmarks of Eric Treacy, the ' railway bishop' who portrayed Settle-Carlisle country in a way that few have equalled. The setting is Skipton, southern gateway to the line. 2-6-4T No. 42492 is departing with a local service on the branch to Colne, closed in 1970.

HOLIDAY EXCURSION

TO

ESHTON HALL.

The Committee of the **KEIGHLEY MECHANICS' INSTITUTION**, beg to announce that they have made arrangements for an Excursion to Eshton Hall, the Residence of **MATTHEW WILSON**, Esq.

On Whit-Monday, May 28th, 1849.

THE PARTY,

ACCOMPANIED BY THE KEIGHLEY BAND,

Will leave the Railway Station at half-past Twelve o'clock and proceed to Skipton, at which place a number of **BOATS** will be in readiness to convey them to Eshton Hall. After spending the Afternoon in visiting the

SPLENDID GROUNDS

&c. &c.

connected with that place, which, through the kindness of **MR. WILSON**, will be thrown open, the Party will return to Skipton, which place they will leave at Eight o'clock.

The Members and Friends, headed by the Band, will leave the Mechanics' Institution in Procession, at Twelve o'clock precisely.

Tickets to Eshton Hall and back;—

First Class, 2s. 6d.—Second Class, 2s.—Third Class, 1s. 6d.

May be had of Mr. Aked, Mr. Hudson, and Mr. Crabtree, Booksellers.

The Male and Female Classes will receive their Tickets at the Institution, on Thursday and Friday Evenings, from half-past Eight to half-past Nine.

Persons intending to join the Party, are requested to purchase their Tickets on or before Saturday Evening, that the Committee may make their arrangements accordingly.

J. L. CRABTREE, PRINTER, KEIGHLEY.

Visitors were flocking to the Yorkshire Dales well before the Settle-Carlisle line was conceived. The railway had been open to Skipton for little more than 18 months when Keighley Mechanics' Institution arranged this grand Whit Monday excursion – complete with band. Passengers simply walked across the road to the Leeds & Liverpool Canal, from where narrow boats would take them to Gargrave and the "splendid grounds" of Eshton Hall.

Bell Busk, one of the attractive half-timbered stations on the "little" North Western Railway, opened in 1849 from Skipton to Ingleton. Here passengers for Scotland changed trains to continue their journey – an arrangement that was far from satisfactory and eventually drove the Midland to conceive its direct route from Settle to Carlisle. Bell Busk was for many years the station for Malhamdale, horse-drawn "conveyances" taking passengers to gaze in awe at Malham Cove and Gordale Scar. (David Joy collection)

Hellifield became an important junction station in 1880 with the opening of the Lancashire & Yorkshire line from Blackburn and Clitheroe. This line-up of locomotives alongside the coaling stage was photographed in October 1937. (David Joy collection)

Hellifield, still with an air of bustle on a summer afternoon in 1960. 'Crab' No. 42833 from Kingmoor shed is heading a Carlisle-Stourton freight past North Junction signal box. Careful scrutiny reveals various Stanier locomotives clustered round the shed on the right. (John M. Hammond)

A 'Crab' 2-6-0 heading south enters the short Stainforth tunnel under the grounds of what is now a youth hostel. (D. Ibbotson)

Derby No. 9, *one of the contractor's locomotives used during the building of th line. The location is believed to be Helwith Bridge.* (Mary Farnell collection)

Settle-Carlisle country personified, with the unmistakable shape of 2,273ft Penyghent in the background. From this viewpoint the mountain has been likened to a crouching lion. Class 40 No.40 094 is crossing the river Ribble near Helwith Bridge with a northbound freight in May 1981. (Gavin Morrison)

Winter has always been a factor on the Settle-Carlisle, most notably in 1947 when the line was blocked for two months by deep snow. Severe problems returned earl in 1963 when this Edinburgh-London sleeper train was engulfed by drifts south of Rise Hill Tunnel. A heroic rescue operation was necessary to get the passengers back to Carlisle.

The highest water troughs in the world were to be found on the remote stretch of line between Rise Hill Tunnel and Garsdale station. Keeping them free of ice in the winter months could be a near-impossible operation. 'Crab' No. 42819 is crossing with an up freight consisting mainly of tan wagons. (J.W. Armstrong Trust)

After years of what was officially described as 'wanton neglect', British Rail found itself facing a huge backlog of maintenance work when the line was reprieved in 1989. This took its most dramatic form with the closure of the route later that year so that work could go on day and night at Ribblehead Viaduct. In such a lonely location, the battery of arc lamps made an eerie sight. (R.W. Swallow)

9F 2-10-0 No. 92019, one of the class most closely associated with the line in the last years of steam, leaves Blea Moor Tunnel with the Long Meg gypsum train. Spoil heaps from the tunnel shafts can be seen on the distant moorland.
(A. Sainty collection/Colour-Rail BRM742)

New era on the Settle-Carlisle. A group of Raleigh International volunteers, building new car parks and fencing at Garsdale station, takes a break to watch Flying Scotsman *storm past on the Guild '92 Steam Special.* (Linda Viney)

Ais Gill Summit, 1,169ft above sea level, where the line leaves the Yorkshire Dales and enters the Eden Valley. A gypsy caravan is an intriguing item on this freight leaving the up refuge siding behind 4F No. 44451 in July 1961.
(Derek Cross)

The afternoon stopping service from Bradford Forster Square to Carlisle came close to the once common concept of a mixed train. It often conveyed more vans than coaches and called at no fewer than 26 stations on a leisurely journey occupying almost four hours. Characteristic 5MT motive power was at the head of the train in August 1964 when it crossed Arten Gill viaduct, one of the most attractive structures on the line. (Roger Bastin)

The Settle-Carlisle now has a more intensive local passenger service than at any time in its history. Most of the workings are by 'Sprinter' units, as seen here in glorious weather in Dentdale. This view well shows the dry-stone walls that are such a feature of the railway – and have been extensively restored in recent years. (Pete Shaw Photography)

SWALEDALE

At the northern end of our region the market town of Richmond stands as a gateway to Swaledale. Further up the valley, and in neighbouring Arkengarthdale, lead was mined for hundreds of years, carried down by horses. With the coming of the railway age it was taken to railheads at Croft and Cowton on what was to be the East Coast Main Line but the provision of a rail connection into the dale was an obvious attraction to promoters.

In 1844 the Great North of England Railway applied for powers to construct a branch from Eryholme Junction (originally Dalton Junction), 5¼ miles south of Darlington, to Richmond. The Act was passed on 21st July 1845 and the 9½-mile branch was opened on 10th September 1846 by what had by then become the York & Newcastle Railway. Intermediate stations were established at Moulton, Scorton and Catterick Bridge.

At Richmond a handsome terminus with overall roof was provided to the design of the well-known York architect G.T. Andrews. The facilities included an engine shed, goods warehouse and small gasworks. The station was located on the opposite side of the Swale from the town, so the railway company built a bridge across the river to give access to it.

Various proposals were floated over the years to extend the line: to Reeth, Hawes and Settle in 1845, to Reeth in 1869, to Muker and Hawes in 1881. Absurdly ambitious schemes were suggested to use the branch as part of a Darlington to Hellifield route and even a link between Barrow-in-Furness and the east coast, but none saw light of day and Richmond remained as far as the railway penetrated into Swaledale.

Though the lead-mining industry declined, another source of passenger and freight traffic came to the Richmond branch with the opening of a large army camp at Catterick in 1915 and a military railway, with a total mileage of some five miles, was built to serve it. At the time of its establishment the Great War was at its height and up to 45,000 men were stationed at the camp at any one time, with some 750,000 passing through it in a year. The military railway acquired a motley assortment of former main line locomotives and stock, though these were disposed of after the end of the war. Catterick Camp was further developed during World War II. There was a passenger service (worked by the LNER) between Catterick Bridge and the Camp, some trains running through to Darlington. A feature of operations for many years was a service of trains in the early hours of Sunday and Monday mornings for soldiers returning from weekend leave.

An interesting signalling experiment took place on the branch in 1911. At this time various systems were being tried which would give an indication in locomotive cabs to the aspect of signals during fog. Vincent Raven, Chief Mechanical Engineer of the North Eastern Railway, devised a system of electrical cab signalling in which steel brushes on the locomotive came into contact with metal ramps between the tracks. When these ramps were energised they gave a continuous indication of the state of the signals. Only locomotives fitted with the necessary apparatus were permitted to work the branch. The system was taken out of use in the early 1920s but it can be counted as one of many steps along the way to the Advanced Warning System in use today and indeed, the Automatic Train Protection envisaged for the future.

Whilst troop trains during the two world wars brought spells of intense activity to the branch, a memorable one-off busy day was on 29th June 1927. The Richmond branch shared with the Wensleydale line the distinction of being chosen by the LNER as a main destination for excursions for observers of the tota eclipse of the sun taking place early that morning. Five special came up to Richmond — two from King's Cross overnight (one including sleeping cars), one from Marylebone and Grea Central main line stations, and one each from Edinburgh and King's Lynn. An additional shunting engine was allocated to the branch for the day, along with two service trains which followed the last special to provide water tanks and gas for the excursions stabled along the up line between Richmond and Catterick Bridge.

The Richmond branch was proposed for closure in th 'Beeching Report' but managed at first to stave off the axe A reasonably busy service — eleven trains either wa Monday to Friday plus an extra 'Saturday night out' working — continued to link Richmond and Darlington until 1969 when o 3rd March the economists finally had their way. Goods traffi continued to Catterick Bridge until the following February, afte which the branch and camp line were lifted. Richmond statio nevertheless continues to give service to the local population — after closure it was converted for use as a garden centre and swimming pool was built on the site of the goods yard!

LNER A5 4-6-2T No.9830 at Catterick Bridge and about to cross the Great North Road with the 7.20pm Richmond—Darlington, led by some NER clerestory coaches, on 22nd June 1947. The A5 class was originally a Great Central Railway design introduced in 1911 for London area suburban services; when the LNER needed additional powerful tank engines for the North Eastern Area shortly after the Grouping, the GC design was adopted and a further thirteen built by Hawthorn, Leslie & Co. of Newcastle in 1925/6 of which No.9830 was the first. In February 1944 munitions being loaded in the station yard exploded, killing twelve people and injuring 102 and badly damaging the station buildings.

The army camp at Catterick was rail connected and generated a substantial volume of freight over the years. On 9th March 1966 LNER K1 2-6-0 No.62041 was working the pick-up goods in the camp sidings and easing over the ungated road crossing under the protection of a flagman, with the shunter riding on the rear steps of the tender. (J.S. Gilks)

RICHMOND

LEFT: *The Richmond branch terminus in 1965. The station building was designed by G.T. Andrews and the roof covered three tracks but only one platform; the other platform was outside the roof to the right and culminated in a horse-loading dock.* (David Sutcliffe)

BELOW: *During a quiet moment at Richmond the train and station staff await custom in front of a large poster advertising the famous Newcastle Brown Ale. After closure the station was converted for use as a garden centre.* (David Sutcliffe)

Darlington shed's L1 2-6-4 tanks were used on Richmond branch services and No.67750 is departing with what appears to be a special carrying express headlamps.
(J.W. Hague/D.V. Beeken collection)

WENSLEYDALE

Wensleydale is a fertile valley with agricultural land bounding on to the River Ure and is noted for its dairy produce — not least its famous cheese. Running east to west through Wensleydale from the East Coast Main Line at Northallerton to the Midland Railway at Hawes Junction (later Garsdale), on the Settle—Carlisle route, was a branch line of some 39 miles built in a curiously piecemeal manner.

The first section took the form of a branch from Northallerton to Bedale, promoted in 1846 by the Newcastle & Darlington Junction Railway, part of the empire of George Hudson, the so-called 'Railway King' of York. At this time the NDJR was leasing the Great North of England Railway (which had built the York—Darlington main line) and soon obtained powers to purchase it. From 27th July 1846 the new company was known as the York & Newcastle Railway which a year later amalgamated with the Newcastle & Berwick company to form the York, Newcastle & Berwick Railway. All this took place while the Bedale branch was under construction but as part of the fall-out arising from the downfall of Hudson it was not fully completed, stopping short at Leeming Lane. It was the YNBR which opened this extent of the branch on 6th March 1848.

The next 11¾ miles to Leyburn were promoted by the Bedale & Leyburn Railway, which was also empowered to complete the remaining original stretch between Leeming Lane and Bedale. The YNBR subscribed to the construction of the line and undertook to work it on completion. The 'missing link' to Bedale was opened on 1st February 1855 but by then the amalgamation of the YNBR, the York & North Midland and the Leeds Northern had taken place which created the mighty North Eastern Railway. The Bedale—Leyburn section was opened to freight on 24th November 1855 and to passengers on 18th May 1856, then in 1859 the local company was formally taken over by the NER.

There were various further proposals to construct railways through Wensleydale as part of schemes for through routes and branches, none of which actually came to fruition. One which came nearer than others was the Hawes & Melmerby Railway Act, passed in 1865. The NER, driven by its desire to keep out competitors, offered to subscribe half the cost but economies forced postponement of the project and when it became necessary to renew its powers, the NER decided instead to go for just the cheaper option of an extension of the existing branch from Leyburn to Hawes. This was authorised in 1870, with the sixteen miles being opened to goods on 1st June 1878 and to passengers four months later.

The final link in the chain came from the west. An 1866 Act of Parliament had given the Midland Railway authority to build its Settle—Carlisle main line and also provided for a 5½-mile branch from Hawes Junction to Hawes where it would meet the NER. The Settle—Carlisle opened in 1876 but it was another two years before the Hawes branch was ready; goods working began on 1st June 1878 and passenger services on 1st October, the same date as the NER's branch opened from Leyburn.

The NER gained running powers from the joint station at Hawes over the Midland down to Settle Junction but only exercised them in respect of passenger trains as far as Hawes Junction. The MR did not exercise its own running powers eastwards to Leyburn other than for occasional excursions.

The Wensleydale branch for the most part lived a quiet life. Passenger traffic in such a rural area was light; the LNER's winter 1934/5 timetable showed five trains on weekdays between Northallerton and Hawes, four of which ran through to what since 1932 had been known as Garsdale, with an afternoon LMS train between Garsdale and Hawes. On Tuesdays only there was an additional morning train from Garsdale to Hawes and back, this being Hawes market day. However, there were peaks in the form of excursion traffic, particularly from the industrial towns of the West Riding and to destinations such as Leeds or Scarborough from the dale's stations. The branch's busiest day, though, was undoubtedly 29th June 1927 when early in the morning a total eclipse of the sun occurred across northern England. Eight specials for eclipse-watchers descended on the Wensleydale branch from King's Cross and Grimsby, Normanton and Castleford, Nottingham Victoria, Scarborough, Leeds, Hull, Norwich and Colchester, and Dewsbury. The trains were stabled along the branch between Leyburn and Aysgarth. At Leyburn two catering trains consisting of a kitchen car and a pair of third class open carriages were positioned in the horse dock and goods siding to provide refreshments.

Milk traffic played an important part in the working of the Wensleydale branch — and not just milk, but also butter and the famous Wensleydale cheeses. In fact, in the 1900s the afternoon Midland goods was instructed "to wait till butter is ready on Tuesdays"! Early in the twentieth century local farmers formed a

Despite the closure of the Wensleydale branch to passengers in 1954, passenger trains continued to appear from time to time in the form of excursions. On 20th May 1967 the ' Three Dales Tour' visited Leyburn behind K1 2-6-0 No.62005 and BR Type 2 diesel No.D5160. (Colour-Rail)

co-operative — the Wensleydale Pure Milk Co. — and in 1905 took the rental of a bottling plant built by the NER at Northallerton. In 1932 milk vans were being despatched to Newcastle and Sunderland, West Hartlepool, Tynemouth, Hull, Dewsbury and London (Finsbury Park and Queen's Park). Mention must also be made of the 'Cream Special', a hand-propelled four-wheel trolley pushed from the dairy into Northallerton station conveying churns and cream cans for the dale's stations.

With the meagre pickings to be had from such a sparseley-populated area, it was no surprise when British Railways withdrew the passenger service between Northallerton and Hawes on 26th April 1954. One train either way continued to ply between Hawes and Garsdale until 16th March 1959 when the former Midland section closed completely, though Hawes continued to receive goods traffic from the Northallerton direction until 27th April 1964.

Stone traffic had been a feature of the Wensleydale branch's traffic since 1908. A number of sidings existed, one of the most important being west of Redmire for the Redmire Limestone Quarry Co., opened in 1920. After local goods traffic was progressively withdrawn from the village stations, traffic from the Redmire quarry kept the branch open until 18th December 1992. Thereafter the branch's future has been uncertain, though there was a revival of traffic in the form of Army tanks when a trial run took place on 15th November 1993. A further train of caterpillar tanks on 9th April 1996 was found to be out of gauge at Northallerton and had to be cancelled. Another run was made on 11th July 1996 and on subsequent dates, though the traffic has now ceased. The story of the Wensleydale branch may still not be finished, however, as there has been a revival of interest (supported by the Wensleydale Railway Association) in the idea of restoring the passenger service through the dale, extending it beyond the existing Redmire terminus to Castle Bolton for the benefit of visitors to this fourteenth century stronghold where Mary, Queen of Scots, was once imprisoned. Time will tell.....

A truly rural scene at Finghall Lane which possessed just a single platform and a crossing box. A single coach suffices for the passengers but J21 0-6-0 No.65038's minimal load is supplemented by a milk tanker. A tethered goat watches its passage in a break from keeping the banks well cropped. (N.E. Stead)

J21 0-6-0 No.65075 calls at Leeming Bar heading a mixed train from Northallerton with milk tankers at the front early in BR days; in the background is the Vale of Mowbray cooked meat factory, another source o local produce traffic. At the east end o the station the Great North Road crossed the railway by a level crossing

Finghall Lane in NER days at a time when small rural stations were lavishl furnished with accommodation and staff who had plenty of time to attend to the horticulture!

The delightfully-named Constable Burton station receives a call from G5 0-4-4T No.67314. Village stations often have eccentric-sounding names but Yorkshire must be unique in having not only Constable Burton but also Burton Constable (on the Hull—Hornsea line)!

By far the busiest day in the life o Leyburn station was on 29th June 1927 when it was host to special excursions run for observers of the solar eclipse taking place early that morning. Here are crowds waiting to board one of the return trains. On the right are catering vehicles for the benefit o passengers and a gas tank for replenishing restaurant car kitchens. (H.C. Casserley)

Another view of the Wensleydale branch's busiest day. D20 4-4-0 No.711 and B16 4-6-0 No.1372 await departure from Leyburn wi a return excursion after the eclipse on 29th June 1927 — mo motive power and carriages than the branch service normally warranted! (H.C. Casserley)

LNER Class Y3 Sentinel shunter runs through Leyburn station with four milk tankers on 27th February 1954. (J.W. Armstrong Trust)

Redmire station in the 1900s with its staff standing guard over their immaculately-tended domain. The station master is presumably the character standing by the bay-windowed office. (NRM 327/86)

G5 0-4-4T No.67345 pulls away from Redmire in the early 1950s. The immediate railway infrastructure has changed little since North Eastern Railway days with a fine assortment of that company's slotted signals, but beyond the single platform can be seen the stone loading plant for a traffic which gave the branch a life into the 1990s. (J.W. Hague)

ʼith stone traffic keeping the branch in business long after the assenger service had ceased, BR Class 37s Nos.37 517 and 37 ı4 pass the closed (but still tidy) Redmire station on 30th ᴅril 1990 with a train of loaded hoppers heading towards orthallerton. (Gavin Morrison)

A new traffic for the Wensleydale branch in the 1990s was tanks for the Army, Redmire being the nearest railhead to the training grounds of Catterick Camp. On 14th February 1997 a couple of tanks await unloading at the new dock with two BR Class 47s Nos.47 213 and 47 033 in attendance. (Gavin Morrison)

A damp day at Hawes station on 6th September 1958 with LMS Class 4 2-6-4T No.42051 on the Garsdale local. There was by then just the one train either way, running in the afternoon, and it has quite a little audience including a boy in wellingtons and some gentlemen in plastic raincoats. In six months this service would pass into history. (Gavin Morrison)

A moment in time captured at Hawes on 19th September 1953. An LMS 2-6-2T is at the head of the 4.25pm to Hellifield and a young lady has been allowed to have a look in the cab!
(J.W. Hague/D.V. Beeken collection)

A main line flyer demoted to secondary duties, ex-NER D20 4-4-0 No.62347 drifts into Garsdale with a train off the Wensleydale branch in the early 1950s. The Midland main line up to Carlisle is to the left of the picture and the up home signal can just be seen to be off for a southbound train which will presumably connect with the Wensleydale local. Despite over 40 years of closure, the course of the branch to Hawes can still be clearly discerned by travellers on the Settle—Carlisle route.
(J.W. Armstrong Trust)

On the Midland section MR 4F 0-6-0 No.43893 (with tender cab) is working hard on the 1 in 50 gradient as it leaves Mossdale Head Tunnel with the 5.10pm Hawes—Skipton Class H freight on 21st April 1954.
(J.W. Hague/D.V. Beeken collection)

LEFT: *North Eastern Railway G5 0-4-4T No.67278 has its tank replenished at Garsdale on 20th February 1954 after arriving with the 9.50am from Northallerton Originally known as Hawes Junction, Garsdale is some three miles from any sizeable settlement and was established as a junction rather than to serve any immediate population. The row of houses beyond the station is railway cottages.* (T.J. Edgington)

RIGHT: *A stone train makes its way dow the Wensleydale branch betwee Redmire and Wensley behind a Class 6 on 28th February 1992. Bolton Castle i in the background.* (David V. Beeker

BELOW: *The famous turntable at Garsdale with its stockade to prevent locomotives being caught by the strong winds which blow at this exposed location. D20 4-4-0 No.62388 takes a spin on 19th September 1953.* (J.W. Hague/D.V. Beeken collection)

Locomotives and Recollec
No 7903 FOREMARKE H
John Cruxon
7812

First published in 2021

British Library Cataloguing in Publication Data

A catalogue record for this book is available from the British Library.

ISBN 978 1 85794 573 7

Silver Link Books
Mortons Media Group Limited
Media Centre
Morton Way
Horncastle
LN9 6JR
Tel/Fax: 01507 529535

email: sohara@mortons.co.uk
Website: www.nostalgiacollection.com

Printed and bound in the Czech Republic

Title page: On 27 June 1959 No 7812 *Erlestoke Manor* is double-heading with No 7903 *Foremarke Hall* up Hemerdon bank. *Peter Gray, Transport Library Collection*

Front cover illustration: At Gotherington on Saturday 14 September 2019 we are celebrating the engine's 70th birthday. On the same day GWR tank No 4270 was celebrating 100 years. *Paul Stratford*

Contents

Acknowledgements

I would like to offer my sincere thanks to all of the photographers who have kindly donated pictures and have agreed to their use for the wellbeing of the engine. We are fortunate that today there is digital technology that has helped turn some very poor black & white as well as early colour pictures into useable images. In this area I would like to offer thanks to Roy Lawrence, who has enhanced numerous pictures and, like me, all for the love of the engine. I must also acknowledge the help given to me by the late Malcolm Ranieri, who, having seen my first few pages, encouraged me to push on. He even contacted everyone he could think of, trying to flush out photographs. It is so sad to report that Malcolm passed away in October 2018, not having seen the finished book. Thank you, Malcolm – RIP my friend. To Jack Boskett, James (Jim) Clarke, and Paul Stratford, thank you for your photographs and support, gents! As with Malcolm, I could not have done this without you.

Where photographs are listed as unknown I have tried to track down and establish the original sources. In some cases a second copy appeared from a different source with new details, allowing me to update my records. If anyone sees an uncredited photograph and can provide the photographer's details and other information, I will happily update my records and future editions of this book.

I would also like to acknowledge my personal thanks to my fellow Directors, Jim Clarke, Ron Alexander and Chris Gee, together with the original restoration team based at the Swindon & Cricklade Railway, who helped turn a Barry wreck into a working locomotive that has now successfully run for more than ten years. There was a time in the early days when myself and Jim Clarke, as Chairman, sat with our wives trying to find the way forward for the engine when support and progress on the project was stalling. The prospect of selling No 7903 was a very serious option to be considered and put to the membership. However, Jim and I with our wives' support decided we would give it one last push to see if we could get things moving. That last push did generate some really good people and a real desire to see No 7903 finished. It may have taken us 22 years in total, but the wait was worth it, and without all their dedication and effort we would not have succeeded.

Likewise I must thank John Hancock, whose engineering skills and knowledge have been with me from the time I took on the Restoration Manager role. Also, thanks to the support team at the Gloucestershire Warwickshire Steam Railway, who helped complete an extensive 10-year major overhaul in just over two years so that she could take part in the May 2016 Steam Gala. A huge thanks to every last one of you.

Finally, in a very strange sort of way I would say thank you to the engine itself. It has brought me into contact with lots of people, including some whose friendship now goes beyond the engine and with whom I have shared some really good times. My wife and I have also travelled the world with some, shared holidays, attended weddings, and had some really memorable times that will stay with us always. For that we are eternally grateful.

The last word of thanks has to go to my wife Margaret, whose support during the good and not so good times was invaluable. When Dad suddenly died in May 1990 I wanted to give it all up. A phone call from my recently widowed mother, prompted by Margaret I am sure, brought me to my senses. Thank you, Flower.

Introduction: My Brush with Steam

Why 'My Brush with Steam'? Well, it simply came to me, yet I feel it sort of fits. Being the son of a BR fireman, one of the last at Bristol to pass out to drive steam, based at Bristol Bath Road and later on St Philip's Marsh, on many occasions we went on our bikes to his place of work to collect his wages. Walking through a shed of 'Castles', freight engines, panniers and tank engines seemed quite natural then. I was probably somewhere around 10 years old. So it must be in the blood! Many years later, when Margaret and I had a family of our own, we were visiting my parents in Bristol when Dad, who was still at work, called to say, 'The shed foreman says you can come down and show Leigh [our son] the HSTs.' So there was my 8-year-old son sitting in the driver's seat of an HST, then walking through the engine room of a power car – not many young boys could claim that they had done that. More than that, though, you could say history was repeating itself.

My original intention when I joined the group trying to rescue No 7903 *Foremarke Hall* from Barry scrapyard in the late 1970s was to be an armchair supporter and not to get actively involved. However, that all started to change on 3 September 1987 when the Restoration Manager suddenly passed away. By then we had moved house and were now living close to Swindon and I had attended a few work days at the Swindon & Cricklade Railway at Blunsdon to help out on the restoration work. In mid-1988 I made a complete U-turn and agreed to take on the role of Restoration Manager.

Right from my very first involvement, and purely for my own interest, I slowly amassed a collection of photographs that had been taken while No 7903 was still working for British Railways. Recently my thoughts turned to those photographs and I wondered if I could turn them into a pictorial story of the life and career of the engine. The intention would be to capture the path that the engine's life had taken from its early use in 1949 to the present day. This book is an attempt at recording my journey with the engine, which I hope readers will find of interest.

I have structured the book into the following sections:

1. Some of the best BR pictures from the collection. I have tried to add a bit of variety as photographers in the 1940s to the 1960s all seemed to focus on the traditional front-three-quarter shot.
2. A smaller section of her time in Barry. Here the issue is that as the engines were stabled so closely together good pictures are quite rare.
3. A selection of restoration photographs. I took quite a few of these myself, but photography is not what I am particularly good at, so finding a representative selection has proved to be a challenge. I have managed to find a few taken by others, which has helped.
4. *Foremarke Hall*'s days in preservation service. Here I have been very fortunate in that I have had some really good pictures donated by very skilled photographers.
5. The next overhaul and beyond.

I hope you enjoy the journey.

John Cruxon
Locomotive Manager, No 4073 *Foremarke Hall*

1 BR days

Of the 330 'Hall' Class locomotives built at Swindon, 71 were known as 'Modified Halls'. These 'Modified' engines were built under the watchful eye of Chief Mechanical Engineer Frederick William Hawksworth at Swindon Works between 1944 and 1950, with No 7903 being one of the last – she was built and listed as completed on 10 May 1949. The total cost, including the tender, is shown on her Swindon history card as £10,565. Initially she went into storage at Swindon awaiting allocation to a shed; that came in July 1949 when on the 27th of that month she was allocated to Old Oak Common.

No 7903 spent the vast majority of her working life based at Old Oak, travelling all over the Western Region and carrying out all the varied duties for which this class of engine was known. In 1961 she did have two very short spells allocated to Southall and Oxford before being transferred back to Old Oak Common. The engine was finally transferred to Cardiff East Dock in October 1963, just prior to withdrawal and sale to Woodham Brothers for scrap. Movement to Barry scrapyard came on 18 August 1964 on trip working No 26.

During her BR working life she managed to accumulate a total mileage of 621,101 miles. The 'Modified Halls' were nicknamed by the footplate crews as 'Greyhounds' as they seemed to be somewhat fleeter of foot than their earlier classmates. In fact, No 7903 distinguished herself in 1951 by deputising for the normal 'Castle' on the Plymouth to Paddington boat train and was the first locomotive to cover the distance in less than 4 hours.

No 7903 is the only surviving '79xx' 'Modified Hall', as the only other survivor, No 7927 *Willington Hall*, is in the process of being converted to a 'County' Class locomotive by the Great Western Society at Didcot.

No 7903 is seen at Cox Green on a stopping passenger on 4 August 1949. Allocated new to Old Oak Common, the locomotive is just four months old. *Photographer unknown*

Here she is stabled at Old Oak Common Shed on 10 May 1952. You can just see a 'King' Class loco buffered up behind. *F. M. Gates*

The caption says that No 7903 is on the 'up stepper' (stopper?) at Iver in Buckinghamshire on 24 April 1952. *Photographer unknown, Transport Treasury Collection*

Above: East Somerton, with the 12.30pm down Minehead on 6 September 1952. The photographer was a very active member in the days of recovering No 7903 from Barry and in the sourcing of numerous parts, including the safety valve bonnet from No 7911 *Lady Margaret Hall*. *Ray Simpson*

Right: Later the same day No 7903 is seen on the 3.50pm up Paddington. *Ray Simpson*

Above: On 13 September 1952 the locomotive is on the 3.06pm down passenger. *Ray Simpson*

Above right: On shed at Oxford, 15 February 1953. *Ray Simpson*

Right: In Sonning Cutting on 19 April 1954. A note says that she is in black livery. *Dick Blenkinsop*

At Oxford on 8 May 1954. *L. B. Lapper, Ken Davies collection*

Above: Leaving Dawlish with a down train on 25 August 1954. *Dick Blenkinsop*

Above right: No 7903 pilots 'Castle' Class No 5095 *Barbury Castle* on the Devon banks at Rattery on 5 July 1955. *R. C. Riley*

Right: Totnes on 1 August 1955. According to Swindon records No 7903 regained a Hawksworth tender on 19 January 1952 having lost her original in September 1951, but by 17 January 1956 she was paired with a Collett tender again. *R. K. Blencowe*

Above: Entering Bath Spa with the 7.30am Paddington to Paignton train on 25 February 1956. *D. Bartlett*

Above right: Entering Bath again on the same day. Strangely the smokebox darts are now in a different position, so did No 7903 come off at Bristol and go on to Bath Road shed for a smokebox clean ready for the return working, with the previous Paignton train going forward behind a Bath Road engine? *Rail On Line Collection*

Right: Another early colour picture shows the locomotive at Twyford on 19 April 1958. *T. Owen, Colour Rail Collection*

Far right: On shed at Swindon, her birthplace, on 22 April 1956. *Ray Simpson*

025
HATHERLEY HALL

Above left: While not a particularly inspiring shot, this is one of the earliest colour pictures I have. It was taken at Old Oak Common shed in May 1956. *Photographer unknown*

Above right: On an empty coaching stock working at West Drayton on 22 March 1959. According to Swindon records No 7903 should be paired with Collett tender No 2555, yet this image shows her attached to a Hawksworth. *Martin G. C. Smith*

Left: On the 'Royal Duchy' at Taunton on 27 July 1958. *Ken Davies, Ken Davies collection*

Below: Seen at Old Oak Common shed on 1 April 1960, *Foremarke Hall* is about three months out from a Heavy General Overhaul at Swindon; she was released back to OOC on 29 January 1960. This particular photograph has two different sources: I believe the photographer is P. H. Groom and it is now part of the G. Parry collection.

Above: Entering Reading station, past a permanent way slack, on 4 May 1959, heading the 10.00am to Birmingham. *J. C. Beckett*

At Old Oak Common shed on 3 July 1960. There are two things quite unique about this picture – do you know what they are? The answers are given at the start of the next chapter. *Dick Blenkinsop*

At Exeter St David's on 9th July 1960, with the 11.40am Paddington to Penzance, running 21 minutes late. *John Hodge*

Above: At Bristol Temple Meads on 27 July 1960, one of the two schoolboys could easily have been me as it was where I went when trainspotting. *A. R. Valentine, ARPS collection*

Above right: Seen at Bath Spa, the headlamp code shows that it's a stopping train, with the chalked '7' indicating that it is heading for Swansea and West Wales, some time in the 1960s. Swindon records suggest that at this time the locomotive would have had a Collett tender attached, which she obviously hasn't got here. *STEAM – Museum of the GWR, Swindon*

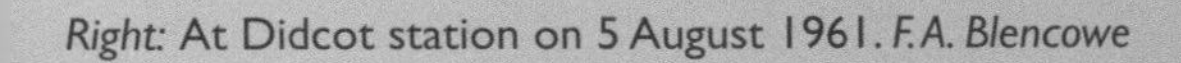

Right: At Didcot station on 5 August 1961. *F. A. Blencowe*

On the Great Central main line heading towards Catesby Tunnel in Northamptonshire on 10 September 1961. *G. Parry, Colour Rail Collection*

Left: At Taunton station some time in 1961. *Photographer unknown, courtesy of RCTS Archive*

Below: Inside Swindon Works, having her last Heavy General Overhaul on 1 July 1962. *STEAM – Museum of the GWR, Swindon*

Below right: Outside Swindon Works, looking as though she is undergoing a steam test. This picture is also dated 1 July 1962 – could it genuinely be later the same day? *A. Ives, ARPS Collection*

At 7.30pm on 2 September 1962 No 7903 takes water at Kingham station with an up freight. The train is about to set back, reason unknown. *Michael Mensing*

At Bruton, between Frome and Castle Cary on the Berks & Hants line, in September 1962. *P.A. Fry*

Passing Steventon with the 7.45am Swindon to Paddington express on 21 September 1962, while *Arlington Grange* is being re-railed. This photograph appears in the book *Signalman's Twilight* by Adrian Vaughan, whose late father, H. O. Vaughan, took the picture. As the caption in the book says, note the informality of the proceedings: shouts of 'Mind yer back!' and engine whistles are all that is being used. No 7903 is about to enter the loop, which has been converted into a passenger train line by a written certificate.

I cannot recall where this particular picture came from, but it is 1962 and the train is a Newbury Races special, the '0' suggesting that it might be a return working to London. It looks as though another 'Hall' Class loco is coupled behind. *Photographer unknown*

Another rare colour shot inside Swindon running shed some time in 1963. *Chris Webb*

Above left: This picture is take from a slide that no longer exists, hence the poor quality. It is dated as 8.30am in April 1963 at Paddington station. I would guess that it is an empty coaching stock movement, as tender engines would rarely run tender-first. *Chris Webb*

Above: At West Ealing, No 7903 heads a freight for the Greenford branch on 21 June 1963. *Don Benn*

Left: Arriving at Paddington from Worcester on 15 June 1963. This early colour image loses quality if further enlarged. *David Christie*

Right: Climbing through the Chilterns south of Saunderton with a Class 8 freight on 28 September 1963. I have had this picture on my study wall for many years and only recently noticed that the smokebox dart handles are not in the correct position. *Brian Stephenson*

Below: Here is yet another case of two photographs taken by two different photographers on the same day, 28 September 1963. No 7903 is almost certainly working the same diagram. *Peter Matcham*

Below right: On 5 October 1963 *Foremarke Hall* heads a down Class C goods at Bradenham between Wycombe and Princess Risborough on the GW&GC Joint line. *Brian Bailey*

On 23 November 1963 No 7903 is seen on shed at Severn Tunnel Junction. She was still allocated to OOC at this time. The headlamp code suggests that she last worked a stopping passenger train. *John Diston*

No 7903 has arrived at Platform 6 at Bristol Temple Meads with the 5.15pm Weston to Bristol stopping train on Wednesday 1 January 1964. It had earlier taken over the 1.45pm Paddington-Weston train from a failed diesel. The unusual headlamps are the consequence of a timed exposure; the top lamp was the stopping train and the two lower lamps were the empty stock from Temple Meads to Dr Day's Carriage Sidings. *Courtesy of Patrick O'Brien/David Nicholas*

Acting as station pilot at Hereford on 20 March 1964, with less than three months to go before withdrawal. *Rail Online Collection*

This is believed to be Old Oak Common shed, on an unknown date. *Photographer unknown, Lens of Sutton Collection*

With what appear to be drums of cylinder oil in the foreground, No 7903 stands at Weymouth shed in an undated scene, with No 5935 *Norton Hall* in the background. No bunded oil tank storage here? *G. Parry collection*

Above: Unfortunately the date and photographer of this picture are unknown.

Above right: In this undated photograph No 7903 is being banked up the Lickey Incline.
Ray Simpson

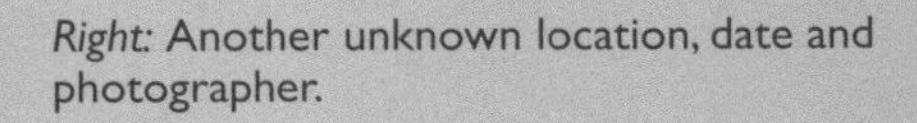

Right: Another unknown location, date and photographer.

Passing Old Oak Common on a parcels train, date unknown. *M. J. Sarah, Colour Rail Collection*

2 Barry scrapyard and Swindon Works

The next collection of pictures, a number of which are undated, are based around the engine's time spent at Barry and its subsequent departure from there. It includes the visit to Swindon Works en route to the Swindon & Cricklade Railway, which was to be our base for restoring No 7903. We were very fortunate in that the late Ivor Huddy, who was a keen member of the Swindon & Cricklade Railway, was also very active in helping us move the locomotive from Barry. His full-time job was a Mechanical Traction Inspector for BR in Swindon Works, so he had all the right skills as well as the right connections for getting things done to make the move happen. His nickname was 'Hot Box Huddy', as he had been called out on more than one occasion to attend to ex-Barry engines that had run hot axle boxes while being towed by rail to their new homes; it was only in later years that everything had to go by road. It was also his suggestion that we timed our moved of No 7903 from Barry so as we could visit Swindon Works Open Day on Saturday 6 June 1981. Delivery to the Swindon & Cricklade Railway was on Sunday the 7th.

Note

The answers to the question of the three engines seen at Old Oak Common shed on 3 July 1960 (page 14) are as follows:

1. All three engines are currently preserved, the 8F being on the Keighley & Worth Valley Railway and No 6023 *King Edward II* at the Great Western Society at Didcot, with No 7903 *Foremarke Hall* at the Gloucestershire Warwickshire Steam Railway, Toddington.

2. All three engines were built at Swindon, as the Works also built some 8Fs. No 48431 is the only surviving Swindon-built 8F.

By 24 October 1965 No 7904 *Foremarke Hall* has been in the yard for 15 months and is still almost intact. The connecting rods have been removed to tow her there, but a lot of the bronze items still appear to be in place, suggesting no serious attention from the Dai Woodham scrap team yet. This was a particularly common view, as I have about three different versions, two taken on consecutive days by different photographers. The original leading/driving coupling rods were later re-acquired from the Great Western Society in a trade swap that suited both parties. *Bob Shepperson*

This undated colour picture is very similar to the previous view. *Photographer unknown*

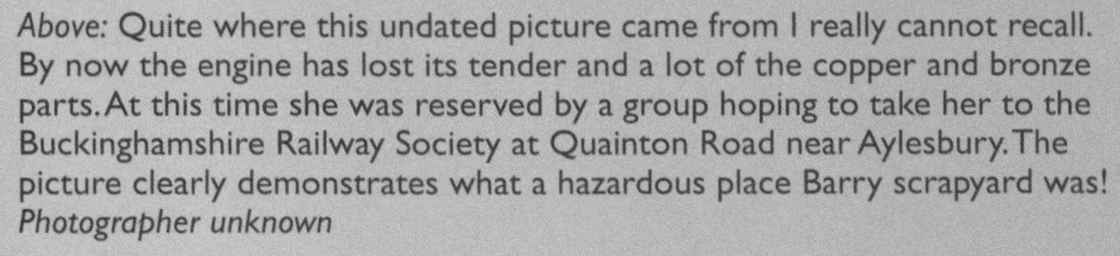

Above: Quite where this undated picture came from I really cannot recall. By now the engine has lost its tender and a lot of the copper and bronze parts. At this time she was reserved by a group hoping to take her to the Buckinghamshire Railway Society at Quainton Road near Aylesbury. The picture clearly demonstrates what a hazardous place Barry scrapyard was! *Photographer unknown*

Above right:: In a similar shot to the previous one, and also undated, now all the cladding has gone as well as the asbestos boiler insulation. No 7903 almost certainly lost the insulation and cladding following a campaign assisted by Robert Adley MP, whose aim was to help save the Barry engines by using his political influence to have all the dangerous materials removed. *Photographer unknown*

Right: Yet another similar and undated picture, but this time showing the other side. No 7903 has a lot of parts missing, including the brake hangers, and the driver's step has been cut off to allow Dai Woodham's men to recover the exhaust injector, which was a very large bronze casting and almost certainly went for scrap. Looking at this now we must have been mad to take it on! *Photographer unknown*

Lloyds Bank Limited
13th April 1981
30-11A
THE BROADWAY NEWBURY BRANCH
20 THE BROADWAY NEWBURY BERKS RG13 1AY
PAID 15 APR 1981
PAY Woodham Bros
Ten thousand three hundred and fifty Pounds only
£10350-00
For FOREMARKE HALL LOCOMOTIVE
Director.
Director.
0165884

Above: Unfortunately by the time we were ready to pay for the engine VAT had been introduced, which pushed up the purchase price. If you look at the date the cheque was presented, it is just two days after Dai Woodham received it.
Ron Alexander/Jim Clarke

Above: In this undated view she has been cleaned up and given a paint job to smarten her appearance. This was done by a team of lads who would go to Barry and generally clean up engines, hoping to entice a buyer. Harry Barber and Mike Cousons were two names that I recall being part of that team, and had even made a fibreglass chimney to improve the engine's appearance. Foremarke Hall Locomotive Ltd had now bought her and her departure was waiting for Dai Woodham's team to shunt the yard and put her in the loading area. *Photographer unknown*

Left: Seen in this undated view is the tender for No 7903 in Barry yard waiting for us to pay for her, followed by a big yard shunt! It was the last of the four Hawksworth tenders to leave the yard; two had gone to a steelworks to be converted to ingot carriers, and the other lived on the Severn Valley Railway for many years but is now running behind another 'Modified Hall', No 6990 *Witherslack Hall*, on the Great Central Railway. *Photographer unknown*

Above: While in the previous shot the tender looks in reasonable condition, this undated view tells a different story and shows what years in the salty Barry air have done. *Photographer unknown*

Above right: Salvation has come! Loco and tender have been shunted onto the loading road ready for departure. Note the spare hand rail in the tender recovered from No 7927 *Willington Hall* with the idea that it would be fitted to our restored engine. Oh how naïve we were! In fact we replaced all the handrails, other than the complex curved bit around the smokebox door; it was easier to replace them than use the original rails, as they were badly corroded. *Ray Simpson*

Right: The contractor that moved most of the locos by road was a company owned by Mike Lawrence; he had an American Mack truck and was famous for moving engines from Barry. Here the late Ivor 'Hot Box' Huddy looks at the loading ramp while second from the left is the late Gordon Titcombe, another ex-Swindon Works man. The date is Thursday 4 June 1981. *Ray Simpson*

Above: Loading begins on the same day. The person bending with his back to the camera is Ivor 'Hot Box' Huddy, who is checking that all the wheelsets engage with the loading ramp. Note the non-authentic smokebox number plate and fibreglass chimney. *Ray Simpson*

Below: No 7903 is safely on the bed of the trailer. The ramp needs to be dismantled and the engine secured to the trailer bed before she can leave the yard. It should be mentioned that her journey from Barry to Swindon was via Gloucester, as the original Severn Bridge could not take abnormal heavy loads. I am told that the tender went across the bridge on its trailer, although technically it was almost certainly too heavy as well. *Ray Simpson*

Above left: On Saturday 6 June 1981 No 7903 is back home at Swindon Works, her place of birth. *Ray Simpson*

Above: The Mack truck stands proudly with No 7903 on the trailer at her place of creation on 6 June 1981. *Author*

Left: We were so pleased to be at Swindon, and genuinely thought we would get inundated with offers of help from the workforce. However, building a 'Hall' in an erecting shop is totally different from trying to do it at a fledgling heritage railway! A lot of the workforce did not share our enthusiasm, as to them it was simply a job. However, the engine has had her original name and number plates fitted just for this occasion. I am standing by the trailer beyond the man with the bag between his legs. *Ray Simpson*

Below: A bit of a tight turn! Note the steam crane boiler lying on its side. *Ray Simpson*

On Sunday 7 June trying to squeeze her into the Swindon & Cricklade Railway was no simple task. What bit of track that had been laid had to be infilled with sleepers to allow the trailer to turn through 90 degrees so that it could be unloaded – that is after it had reversed down the road and through the narrow entrance. *Ray Simpson*

With both trailers on site, the unloading can commence. *Ray Simpson*

Once again the late Ivor Huddy and the late Gordon Titcombe watch as No 7903 is slowly lowered down the ramp, this time onto the Swindon & Cricklade Railway. *Ray Simpson*

Engine and tender are safely unloaded at Blunsdon on the Swindon & Cricklade Railway, awaiting the long haul of restoration. The date is not recorded. *Author*

3 The restoration begins

The following selection of photographs will hopefully give a flavour of the initial restoration from Barry scrapyard condition to working locomotive. The overhaul took 22 years 2 months to complete, and involved a lot of hard work often in totally unreasonable working conditions. We were a lot younger and very naive then, so were game to tackle anything! It has to be said that while I took on the Restoration Manager role in 1987, a lot of preparatory work had been done by Adrian (Ade) Scutts, Phil Preston, Dave Titcombe and others. By 1987 the engine was back on its wheels and bogie, having all been thoroughly cleaned and painted. The wheelsets had been to Swindon Works for tyre and journal profiling and the axleboxes had been given some attention to make them fit for reuse. In addition, lots of parts had been sourced and general cleaned and painted.

At this time Swindon Works was closing down and through Ivor Huddy we were offered a set of tender frames for £250, which we subsequently bought and moved to the Swindon & Cricklade Railway. They had been modified to carry crane test weights within the Works, but were substantially more complete then those of the tender we had brought out of Barry. The axleboxes had all their bearings and underkeeps, and all the mechanical parts of the brake gear were in place. Most importantly, the frames had little or no corrosion so needed very little repair to the steelwork. The old tender frames were sold and have subsequently been overhauled and now run behind No 5043 *Earl of Mount Edgecumbe* on the main line.

Having moved to Hungerford with my work in 1985, I started to spend some time working with Ade, the first task being to recover the set of tender frames from a disconnected siding at Blunsdon. This is where I will start this section, as soon after I took over the restoration Ade Scutts suddenly passed away. I decided to focus on the tender and put the engine on the back burner for a while as I understood how the tender worked – the engine was a different matter. While doing the tender I could build up my own knowledge and understanding of what made the engine go and what parts we needed to find, get made or overhauled. I also needed to develop a plan so that the restoration could progress in a continuous way. Readers should remember that some replacement parts had to be made new and sometimes the lead times could be years as we waited for enough demand to generate a production run. Here I have to say that my good friend John Hancock became invaluable; not only did he make Great Western fittings for a living, but he could also keep me posted on what new parts were coming up in the near future. He also steered me in the right direction in terms of what areas to tackle and when. Without his help and guidance the restoration job would have been significantly harder and very likely not to the same high standard. We refer to him these days as the 'Great Western Helpline'.

A small footnote to the 2020 winter maintenance of the engine and tender. We decided to inspect the tender lubrication pads for the axles, and the fact that we found a faulty bearing waiting to give us grief was one thing. However, the other was that when we measured the axle bearing face it confirmed that the tender was running on new axles. So, a Hawksworth tender being used in the works for carrying crane test weights was running on brand new or refurbished wheelsets, and both axles and tyres were a brand-new size!

The tender

These are the tender frames that we brought out from Barry. The tank and wheelsets have been removed and the frames are ready for some attention. *Colin Jacks collection*

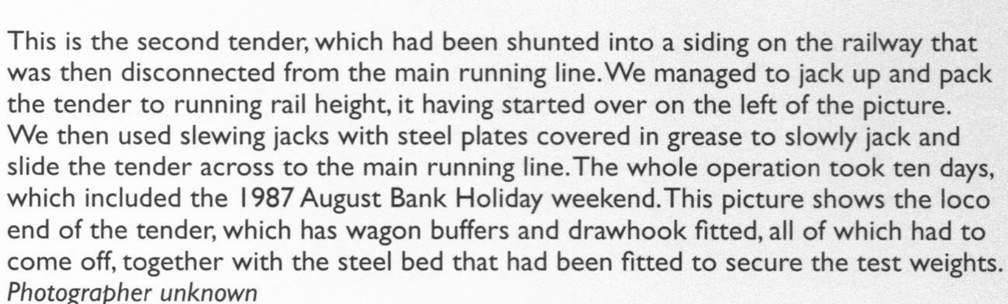

This is the second tender, which had been shunted into a siding on the railway that was then disconnected from the main running line. We managed to jack up and pack the tender to running rail height, it having started over on the left of the picture. We then used slewing jacks with steel plates covered in grease to slowly jack and slide the tender across to the main running line. The whole operation took ten days, which included the 1987 August Bank Holiday weekend. This picture shows the loco end of the tender, which has wagon buffers and drawhook fitted, all of which had to come off, together with the steel bed that had been fitted to secure the test weights. *Photographer unknown*

The condition of the top of the tank was seen earlier, and this view shows the front, with the footplate floor area removed. As can be seen, there is not much prospect of the tank holding water. In a similar operation to that shown in the previous picture, we needed to extract the tank to get it into the car park ready for some specialist repair work. *Colin Jacks collection*

Above: Not a good-quality photograph, but it shows the tank being winched across to the running line in the summer of 1988, where our boiler trolley took it down to the car park. Gordon Titcombe leans on the tender while the rest try their hardest to pull the tank across. *Author*

Above right: Another poor-quality picture, but the tender is now safely loaded onto the boiler trolley ready to be manhandled down the running line to the car park, where it can be loaded onto road transport. *Author*

Right: On Saturday morning the tank has been loaded onto a trailer to go away for the major structural repair work. J. D. Bracey is a local farming and transport company from Lambourn in Berkshire, and I managed to get them to move the tank for us at a significantly reduced cost. The tank sat on the trailer over the weekend and was delivered on Monday morning to the place of repair. *Author*

Above: The tank is lifted by crane ready to be installed onto the tender frames on Friday 2 March 1990, with Nick Peppitt holding the steadying rope. You can see that we had a tidy workplace area! *Chris Gee*

Ron Alexander was one of No 7903's Directors and had the tender tank at his factory for some serious repair work. The tender top has been replaced and the coal space has had some new steel added to strengthen the sides. The date is early 1990.

The arrangement with Ron's company directors was that all structural work would be done, leaving us the cosmetic work to do. Note my crude attempt at publicity on the tank for its journey from Swindon! *Author*

Here is the front view, and it can be seen that a significant amount of work has been done; potentially the tank might now hold water. *Author*

Right: Nick Peppitt and Mick Tiddy help to guide the tank onto the ex-Swindon set of tender frames, which we had now returned to normal tender condition. *Chris Gee*

Above: Nick Peppitt and I are replacing all the rotten or missing pipework that runs under the tender; on this occasion, a Sunday morning during the winter of 1990/91, we are making up the missing steam heating pipework. We must have been mad – just look at the weather! *Author*

Below: In the late summer of 1991 the tender is now in an almost finished state. The temporary scaffolding erected by Chris Gee, Director and major shareholder, and his small team to gain access to the tender tank sides is being dismantled. This was a massive boost to everyone to see such a large bit as good as finished. *Author*

The engine

Here can be seen the level of dismantling that took place in what can only be described as a siding. The engine had previously been jacked up higher and placed on sleepers to allow the wheels to be refitted. Now work is being done to the bogie axleboxes. Although all this looks very primitive, even crude, the engine ran until 2011 on the main axleboxes, and until 2013 on the bogie axleboxes, so the quality of what was done was sufficient to get her working well. Behind the engine can be seen the boiler, and the next big challenge awaiting us. The date of this scene would be the spring of 1987. Rewheeling, led by the then Restoration Manager Adrian Scutts, was finished in the summer of that year. Tragically, Adrian died in September 1987.
Photographer unknown

Here in the late autumn of 1987 we have a set of frames safely mounted back on its wheels and showing signs of progress. The next major task was to move the boiler and frames to a better location in order for us to work on them more safely and easily. *Author*

This picture shows the boiler having been sandblasted by the restoration team and given a coat of protective silver paint. It also clearly shows the expansion of the Swindon & Cricklade Railway in that the running line is now extended well past the boiler, making access by a crane impossible. This was the challenge we had to overcome – for the boilersmith to be able to do the work, the boiler had to be in a more accessible workplace. Fellow Director and fundraiser Chris Gee took on a team leading the challenge, as will be shown in the next few pictures, dating from late 1988 through to late 1989. *Chris Gee*

The issue with trying to move the boiler was its lack of stability, and visible here are two securing chains, firmly anchored to the ground. Under the smokebox are two yellow lifting beams, which are firmly bolted to it; there is also a chain anchored through the firehole door, stopping the whole thing from sliding forward. *Jim Clarke*

Left and below left: These two pictures, dated Sunday 26 November 1989, clearly show the front and rear view of the boiler. The securing chains are in place to prevent any sudden movements while the four jacks under the smokebox lifting beams are slowly pumped up, lifting the front end of the smokebox vertically. You can clearly see the rails that Chris and his team have laid up to and under the boiler so that our boiler trolley can be rolled under the raised smokebox and boiler barrel when ready. *Both Jim Clarke*

Below: The boiler trolley is on the immediate left. Two U-shaped frames were made out of heavy-duty channel by Nick, who is a skilled welder among many other things; one is standing on the running line the other is lying on the boiler trolley – their purpose will be seen in the next picture. Everything is being double-checked before we attempt to roll the trolley under the boiler. *Jim Clarke*

Above: After a long hard day the boiler is finally mounted on the trolley and therefore mobile. You can see the large 'U' frames holding the boiler on the trolley and stopping any sideways movement, the two securing chains keeping the boiler firmly in place. For the first time that day the team can relax and chat! *Jim Clarke*

Above right: A few weeks later we are on the move to the car park via Blunsdon station. *Jim Clarke*

Right: At Blunsdon station the smokebox sign is a bit out of order, as the boiler is definitely on the move. On the extreme right is Roy Dixon, who has been a shareholder and supporter right from the early days to the present time. *Jim Clarke*

Above: The boiler sits in its new home in the car park, where Chris Gee and his team have already started to build a temporary tent over it to allow the contracted boilersmith to work in the dry. *Author*

Above right: In the late spring of 1991, and with the boiler now firmly cocooned from the weather, Pete Gransden, our boilersmith, starts the task of overhauling the boiler. *Author*

Right: In the spring of 1991, with the boiler and the tender in the car park, we moved the loco's frames to the car park as well to make one localised work area. We positioned the tender behind the engine and the boiler in front, so we now had a semblance of a locomotive. *Author*

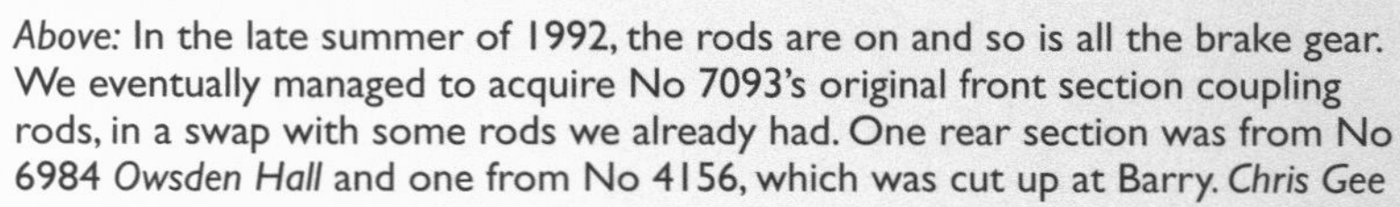

Above: In the late summer of 1992, the rods are on and so is all the brake gear. We eventually managed to acquire No 7093's original front section coupling rods, in a swap with some rods we already had. One rear section was from No 6984 *Owsden Hall* and one from No 4156, which was cut up at Barry. *Chris Gee*

Above right: With the main firebox repair work completed by the boilersmith, we took the decision at the end of 1993 to send the boiler to Swindon Works for them to make a full set of boiler cladding. With the boiler out of the way and the temporary tent removed, the frames are now on the buffer stops in the car park, where we set about fitting the slidebars, crossheads and pistons during 1994 – long, slow and painful work. *Author*

Right: The boiler is inside Swindon Works with the barrel crinoline rings already made and the complex firebox cladding under way. Chris has rubbed down the smokebox and is giving it a coat of black gloss in the summer of 1994. *Author*

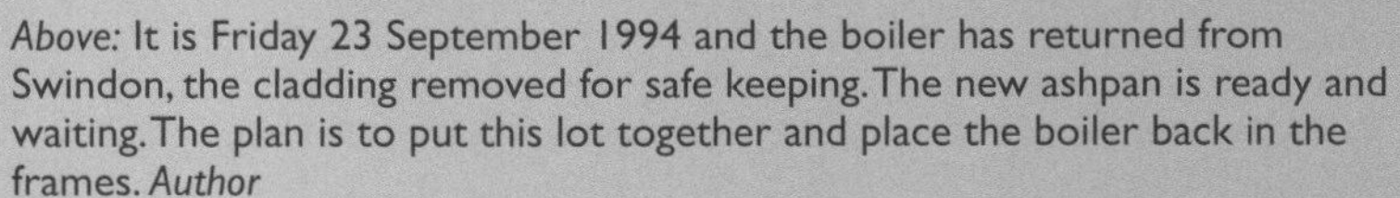
Above: It is Friday 23 September 1994 and the boiler has returned from Swindon, the cladding removed for safe keeping. The new ashpan is ready and waiting. The plan is to put this lot together and place the boiler back in the frames. *Author*

Above right: Two key members of the restoration team, Nick Peppitt and Don Asher, share a conversation now that the ashpan is finally fitted and we are ready to lift the boiler into the frames. *Jim Clarke*

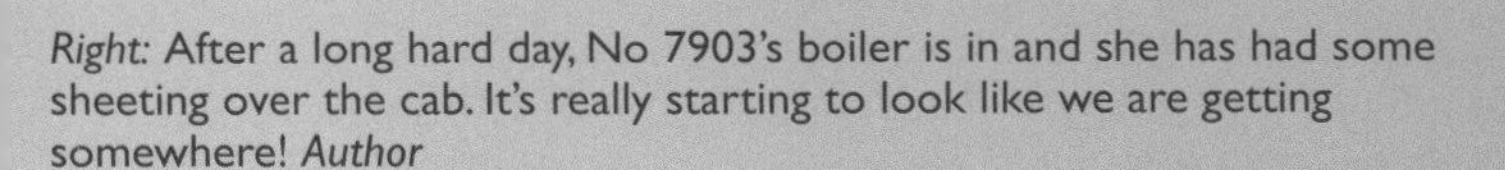
Right: After a long hard day, No 7903's boiler is in and she has had some sheeting over the cab. It's really starting to look like we are getting somewhere! *Author*

With the crane gone, on Friday 23 September 1996, it is time for a team photograph taken by Jim Clarke (it was a timed shot, giving him enough time to dash into the picture). On the engine, left to right, are Chris Gee, John Cruxon, Roy Dixon and Paul Tomes; on the ground, Nick Peppitt, Don Asher, Jim Clarke and Mick Tiddy. One happy team!

Left and below left: These two pictures show the difference we have made. The first is a picture I was sent showing the cab as it was at Barry, while the second one shows the same area as we piped up the backhead ready for her first steaming. This is early 2000, and it can be seen that we are also safely inside Hayes Knoll shed. Being under cover made a massive difference to the way we worked, and prevented our work being undone by the weather. *Photographer unknown/author*

Below: A water test on the tender tank is taking place, as we had a few minor leaks to address. The engine is now getting to look like being complete. This was during one of our work weeks in September 2001. '38xx' Class 2-8-0 No 3845 sits alongside. *Author*

It is now 2002 and after some general cleaning and painting No 7903 was displayed at the Swindon & Cricklade Railway's Summer Vintage Rally. She has been towed down from Hayes Knoll shed and is on display near the Whistlestop Café; she is almost complete and ready for the boiler to be lifted back out of the frames for hydraulic and steam testing. *Author*

Left: The boiler goes back onto the boiler trolley for the last leg of the hydraulic and steam testing. *Jim Clarke*

Below left: Having satisfactorily passed its hydraulic examination, the boiler is seen on test on 11 June 2003. *Author*

Top right: Now with the engine almost complete and nearly ready for her final 'in frames' boiler inspection, Paul and Adam Tomes decide that they will give her a spruce-up with a coat of green paint. This is late on a Sunday evening in September 2003. It is fair to say that this father and son team made a massive contribution to the restoration; both are highly talented with their hands and were highly valued members of the restoration team. *Author*

Right: It is now 18th September 2003 and the engine is fully back together and being readied for her first official steaming and sign-off by the boiler inspector. The crane has just loaded a bag of coal, the first in the tender for about 39 years! *Jim Clarke*

Back on Hayes Knoll shed, No 7903 is raising steam and boilersmith Pete Gransden has a ladder ready to make the final adjustments to the safety valves. *Jim Clarke*

John Hancock fills the hydrostatic lubricator for the first time. In fact, John made the lubricator for us. *Jim Clarke*

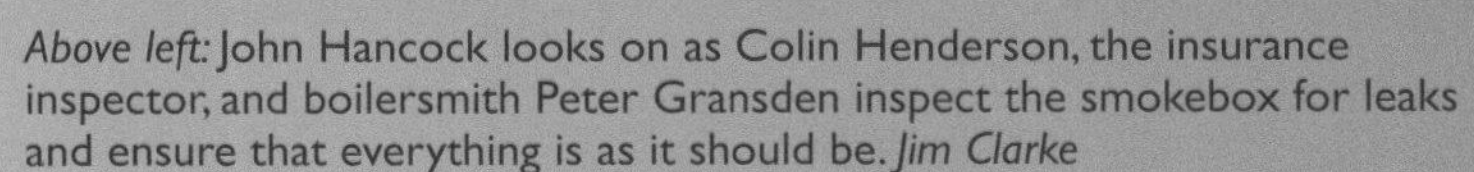

Above left: John Hancock looks on as Colin Henderson, the insurance inspector, and boilersmith Peter Gransden inspect the smokebox for leaks and ensure that everything is as it should be. *Jim Clarke*

Above: The late Den Kelly keeps a watchful eye on me as Adam Tomes (extreme right) keeps an eye on the fire. *Jim Clarke*

Left: With the boiler examination successfully concluded, we have reversed No 7903 off shed and collected a brake van, and the engine has just moved herself into Hayes Knoll platform. While being slightly biased, I have to say that she moved so easily you would have thought she had only stopped the day before. I am the one in the green overalls, and the gentleman nearest the engine on the platform is photographer and shareholder the late Ray Simpson. *Jim Clarke*

THE
BRISTOLIAN
7903

Left: On 20 September 2003 No 7903 pulls her first train as part of the Swindon & Cricklade Railway's 25th Anniversary. The headboard is a personal item, as I'm a Bristolian by birth so it gets the occasional outing. *Jim Clarke*

Right: It is 12 October 2003, the occasion of the engine being renamed and dedicated back into traffic at the Swindon & Cricklade Railway. The renaming was carried out by the children and headmaster from Foremarke Hall School near Derby. *Jim Clarke*

Left: On 12 October 2003 we took a Restoration Group photograph with some of the team. On the platform and engine, left to right, are Jim Clarke, Mike Rennie, John Cruxon, Adam Tomes, Paul Tomes and Roy Dixon; on the track are Chris Gee and Adrian Dorraine. *Jim Clarke*

In the months following No 7903's initial steaming we spent time correcting all the minor snags, then Christmas 2003 saw her successfully pull the 'Santa' trains for the Swindon & Cricklade Railway. In the spring of 2004 we commissioned a small team of contract painters to totally repaint the engine and tender and fully line her out; here she is freshly towed out of the shed for a few of us to see and, I suppose, declare the restoration finally completed. *Steam Railway* magazine called her the 'Brunswick Beauty'. *Author*

4 Stretching her legs in preservation

Following the final painting and another day in service at the Swindon & Cricklade Railway, it was time to move No 7903 to the Gloucestershire Warwickshire Steam Railway. The reason behind this move was quite simple. Having restored her and being fully aware of the costs that go with it, I and my fellow directors were aware that the railway could not offer the sort of steaming fees we needed to build up a fund for her next overhaul. Yes, we were already thinking about her next overhaul before she had done any real work. This insight was fuelled by our good relationship with the Erlestoke Manor Fund, which had vastly more experience with engine operations than we had and were good enough to give us some insight into what was needed. From there we had already been approached by three 'premier league' railways all touting to take on No 7903 as part of their home fleet. I have to say that as the GWSR at Toddington was the closest of the three; their contact man offered us a good deal and was very helpful and obliging, so it soon became the preferred choice. A visit to the railway by Jim Clarke and myself to see for ourselves, together with a footplate ride, helped cement the deal.

In May 2004 No 7903 was one of the stars of the GWSR's Steam Gala and, apart from guest visits elsewhere, has remained there ever since. Currently she has visited the Severn Valley Railway and the Llangollen Railway, and has attended an Old Oak Common Open Day as well as celebrated an Open Day with the new-build 'Saint' at the Great Western Society at Didcot. We are always open to invitations, but the needs of the GWSR comes first, as that is what our contract stipulates. I hope this book will begin to demonstrate how much time and energy has gone into getting her up and running and performing reliably day in and day out. To be honest, if the engine is in service why would I want her elsewhere when I can be in control of her on the GWSR? As I have always said, we are open to offers but they have to be very worthwhile and realistic.

The following selection of pictures is predominately GWSR-based, but I have chosen those that reflect some of the various jobs that No 7903 has done during her first boiler ticket in preservation.

On 6 May 2004 we are getting ready for her first trip to Cheltenham light engine to see how she would perform – her journeys at the Swindon & Cricklade Railway had been less than a mile each way, while Cheltenham was a round trip of 19 miles. *Author*

Left: On the same day, after six stops and no problems, No 7903 arrives safely at Cheltenham. *Author*

Below left: Unbeknown to us we had been spotted on our empty coaching stock runs by local photographer Chris Smith. He has since become a fireman on the GWSR and a supporter of not only the steam department but also No7903. Chris has been my fireman on quite a few occasions and it is always a pleasure to spend the day with him working the engine.
Chris Smith

Below: This is No 7903's first day in traffic at the GWSR, at the May 2004 Gala. On the right is the driver for the day, Andrew Meredith. *Courtesy of the GWSR*

Above: On 27 February 2005 the light almost makes the engine look as though she is black! This looks very much like an 'Elegant Excursions' dining train and, checking the date, it is a Sunday, which is when the dining train ran. The location is coming off Chicken Curve at Winchcombe. *Chris Smith*

Right: Here No 7903 is in the company of *Foxcote Manor* on a visit to the Llangollen Railway for their Summer Gala in 2005. Harry Barber, who was an active member of the Barry Action Group and who helped do some cosmetic work to No 7903 while in the scrapyard, now lives in Llangollen, and he got to drive her at the Gala, as he is a steam driver there. To say he was chuffed is an understatement! *Paul and Adam Tomes*

Left: In another image taken at the Llangollen Gala, No 7903 is matched with a Collett tender; this was because it was spare at the Llangollen Railway at the time and it meant that the railway only had to pay transport for the engine. Her own tender remained at the GWSR, Toddington. *Paul and Adam Tomes*

Right: Hauling a freight at the GWSR Gala on 15 May 2005. *Paul Stratford*

Below right: GWSR driver and Foremarke volunteer Adrian Dorraine gives Jim Clarke, Chairman of 7903 Ltd, guidance on driving her on the occasion of a supporters' day on 25 August 2006. It's Jim Clarke's camera, but we're not sure who pressed the shutter!

Below: On 24 September 2005 No 7903 is caught on camera at Eardington station while on a visit to the Severn Valley Railway. *Dave Hill*

Left: A team shot taken on the same day. *Jim Clarke*

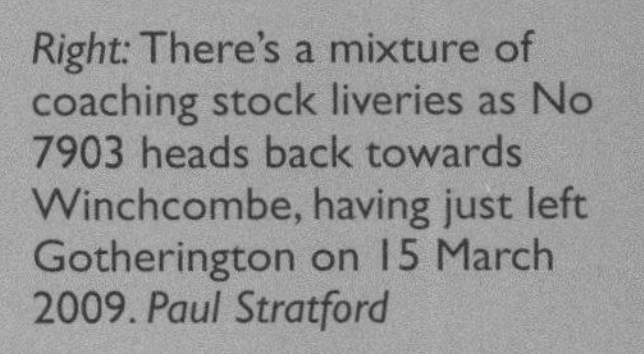

Right: There's a mixture of coaching stock liveries as No 7903 heads back towards Winchcombe, having just left Gotherington on 15 March 2009. *Paul Stratford*

Left: Quite a rare sight: No 7903 at the head of a ballast train on 14 April 2008. *Chris Smith*

Right: Just leaving Gotherington on 2 April 2012. As Gotherington signal box is switched out and not in use, the signal in the distance is set for the return journey through the platform road and not the loop. *Jack Boskett*

Above: Departing from Gotherington for Cheltenham on 6 April 2012. At this time the GWSR was split into two parts due to a major landslip at Chicken Curve, Winchcombe. *Jack Boskett*

Top right: Heading out of Gotherington towards Cheltenham on 11 April 2012. *Paul Stratford*

Right: A special inaugural train traversed Chicken Curve on 30 October 2012 to mark the official reopening of the line following the total rebuild of the embankment after the disastrous landslip during the winter of 2010/11. Engine cleaner and 'King of the Wood Store' Roger Burrows looks out from the cab. The writer is at the controls with Steve Oddy firing. *Malcolm Ranieri*

Right: Leaving Gotherington for the last time prior to her 10-yearly overhaul on 29 December 2013. 'The Cruxonian' headboard was made as a present for me by my good friend Don Asher on my retirement, and featured on my retirement train. The smokebox artwork is by Ben Evason. *Jack Boskett*

Below: No 7903 is pictured on Stanway Viaduct on the way back to Toddington on 2 April 2013. *Jack Boskett*

5 The next overhaul and beyond

With the first ten years' running completed, or to be accurate ten years and three months, as we had obtained a boiler ticket extension to the end of the year, we had the long task of overhauling the engine once again. Fortunately we had already had the wheelsets and axleboxes overhauled at Tyseley in 2011 and the valves were rebored and new rings fitted, again by Tyseley, only this time the work was done at Toddington in the winter of 2012/13. So that work would not need doing on this overhaul.

So the boiler had to be lifted out and shipped to Tyseley Locomotive Works for a full overhaul, including all new tubes, superheater elements, front tube plate and a new smokebox door ring. In the meantime, at Toddington we organised a good clean of the frames and repainting as well as extraction of the exhaust pipes from the exhaust box, which is located under the smokebox saddle. We removed and cleaned all the connecting and coupling rods and also any rust pits or marks we had missed during the first restoration.

The comprehensive list of work to be undertaken was as follows:

1. Completely replace front drawhook, coupling shackles and crossheads with spindle having its thread dressed back to parallel
2. All coupling rods cleaned and buffed up together with overhaul of bearings. including new big-end bushes
3. New gudgeon pins
4. Overhaul of front bogie, including tyre turning
5. Major repairs to exhaust pipes
6. Full boiler overhaul by Tyseley Locomotive Works
7. Overhaul and annealing of all footplate copper pipework
8. New ashpan, including ashpan sprinkler; control valve mounted in cab
9. New steam heat pipework under cab
10. Make up and fit all correct unions and fittings for engine-to-tender vacuum connections
11. Overhaul all cab fittings
12. New engine drawbar pin

In addition, there was all the usual painting, cleaning and general repair work. It is worth saying here that without the help of the first-class team at Toddington, there is no way we would have completed the overhaul in the time we did, two years and five months. Each and every one of them played a significant part, for which I am very grateful.

By 8 February 2014, when this picture was taken, the dismantling of No 7903 was well under way. *Author*

Above: With the boiler removed and away to Tyseley for overhaul, on 14 October 2014 the lads set about cleaning up all the coupling and connecting rods to polish away the pits and rust spots that we had failed to remove first time. Steve Jones, second from left, set the standard very high, so many weekends of rubbing and polishing took place. Left to right are Sean Neilsen, Steve Jones, Dan Wigg and Phil Grange. *Author*

Above right: With the exhaust pipes removed from the engine, Martin Ryan sets about trying to remove years of oil and rust so as we can see the real condition of the pipes. The small curved pipe in the middle is the exhaust steam feed to the exhaust injector; this would be removed and blanked off as we had not fitted an exhaust injector. *Author*

Right: Here are the two exhaust pipes from the driver's-side cylinder block. The two pipes, together with the two from the other side, sweep together to form the base of the blastpipe. As can be seen, there are holes in the pipes that allow exhausting steam from the valve chests to escape into the exhaust box rather than go up the chimney. During this overhaul we had decided we had to investigate with a view to repairing or replacing; this meant that once the boiler had been removed the smokebox saddle plate could be removed to open up the exhaust box. This picture shows what we found. The oil and muck at the bottom was the residue of steam oil from the escaping steam. The next task was to remove the exhaust pipes from the engine.

Right: This is the front end of the boiler on the 28 September 2015 with the new tubeplate fitted, together with all the small tubes. If you look at the front of the firebox you can see that we have also replaced a lot of the front platework as well, up to the white line; this was done rather than patch-repair the cracked areas. *Author*

Above: Here are the repaired exhaust pipes, which have also been heat-treated to stress-relieve the assembly following extensive repairs to the holed areas. The steel jig is to hold the four exhaust flanges in perfect alignment and prevent any movement, as they have to accurately align with the four ports of the two cylinder blocks. It can clearly be seen that the exhaust injector feed has been cut and blanked off. *Adrian Grimmett*

Above right: On 27 December 2014 the exhaust pipes were put back into the exhaust box and the smokebox saddle refitted and bolted back down. All the parts were freshly repaired, cleaned and painted. *Author*

Right: In this November 2014 image you can see the extent of the boiler plate replacement work. The repair work to the backhead is known as a 'Swindon ¾ backhead' and is a repair that was commonly carried out by Swindon Works. We also replaced all the side steelwork that sits inside the frames when the boiler is fitted to the engine. The large chunk of steel around the bottom is called the foundation ring. *Author*

Right: At Tyseley on 6 January 2016, with the boiler mounted on a rail wagon and filled with water, John Pedley, one of the overhaul team, sets about lighting the first fire for steam testing. The bits of tin around the base of the firebox are to stop any cold draughts getting into the boiler. *Author*

Above: No 7903 finally arrives back at Toddington from Tyseley on 10 March 2016 following its ten-year overhaul. *Jim Clarke*

Above: Ten days later, on 20 March, the chimney is on and the two main steam pipes fitted, together with their cladding. Work is now under way to refit all the copper pipes that run along the boiler before the boiler insulation and cladding can be refitted. The white stuff on the running board is the ceramic blanket insulation that we used to lag the steam pipes, and will be fitted around the boiler. *Author*

Above right: On 9 May 2016 painting is well under way. We had done quite a lot of the preparation work ourselves, but we employed contract painters for the vast majority of preliminary and final painting. The top coat of green is on and the smokebox is in undercoat. At this stage painting of the tender was also well advanced. *Tom Halford*

Right: With the painting finished and now sporting the last style of BR logo, on 18 May 2016 No 7903 is raising steam ready for her first round of testing. In the right background two of the overhaul team enjoy a cup of tea. *Author*

Left: On Saturday 28 May 2016 Tina Sutton is my first official fireman with No 7903 back in traffic. I am sure she won't mind me saying that she is rather petite in height, but don't be fooled – she is an extremely good fireman. *Will Grimmett*

Below: Now with the 'Cornishman' headboard and train reporting number frame, on 28 May 2016 No 7903 heads towards Gotherington hauling her first service train following overhaul. *Malcolm Ranieri*

Far left: On 23 May 2016 No 7812 *Erlestoke Manor* once again double-heads with No 7903 into Winchcombe station. This was a test run for No 7812 prior to the May Gala weekend. *Dan Wigg*

Left: On 29 May 2016 No 7903 waits to depart from Platform 1 at Toddington on day two of the Gala. *Jack Boskett*

Below: A stunning shot of No 7903 as she passes Didbrook on 18 May 2017. *M. Ranieri*

Near Manor Lane, also on 18 May 2017. *Malcolm Ranieri*

Above left: Heading to Winchcombe on 5 July 2017, No 7903 passes Hayles Abbey Halt. The halt had recently been completed and opened to the public as a request stop. In 2018 it became a request stop for all service trains, and is quite well used by walkers. *Malcolm Ranieri*

Above: After 57 years, Nos 7903 and 6023 meet up again at Old Oak Common depot on 2 September 2017. The roundhouse and turntable are long since gone, but both engines have been dressed to reflect their previous meeting on 3 July 1960. *Jack Boskett*

Left: At Old Oak Common on the same day, both engines are now dressed for the show. *Jack Boskett*

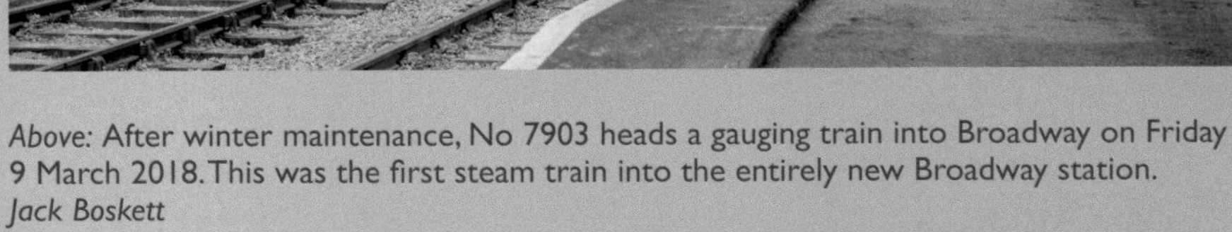

Above: After winter maintenance, No 7903 heads a gauging train into Broadway on Friday 9 March 2018. This was the first steam train into the entirely new Broadway station. *Jack Boskett*

Above right: Here the two ex-Old Oak Common engines reunite for the third time, this time at the GWSR Steam Gala on 27 May 2018. *Jack Boskett*

Right: At a Gotherington stop during the GWSR May Gala in 2019, here again are the two engines with which I got involved in the very early days, towards the end of the 1970s. The first engine, No 6023 *King Edward II*, was the very first engine group I joined, set up to rescue it. Quite what went wrong I don't really know, as I was not that active within the management of the group at the time. However, the group reformed and took up the option on No 7903 *Foremarke Hall*. I wonder how many involved in the preservation game can say that they drove the two engines they were involved with at Barry on the same day some 38 years later? Left to right are myself, Steve Jones my fireman, and Ben Evason, the morning driver of the 'King'. Steve and I became the crew of the 'King' in the afternoon; the morning fireman had been Ray O'Hara.

Above: During 25 the May 2019 Steam Gala No 7903 pilots No 6023 *King Edward II* into Gotherington station. *Mike Wathen*

Right: I thought I would end the book with this photograph, as it is almost certainly where my interest in steam comes from. Dad is sitting on the fireman's seat looking back for the 'right away' from the guard. The picture is undated but was taken at Chippenham station with 'Castle' Class No 5052 *Earl of Radnor*; like No 7903 it has a Hawksworth tender attached.
The late Kenneth Leach